"Informative, practical, and authenti[...] [...]rience of being safe, seen, and soothed while gently helping [...] become the parent their LGBTQ+ kid needs them to be."

—Tina Payne Bryson, LCSW, PhD, New York Times Bestselling co-author of *The Whole-Brain Child* and *No-Drama Discipline*, Founder of The Center for Connection

"I can't think of more important subject to tackle with candor, simplicity, and grace. This book should be on every parent's nightstand."

—Liz Vaccariello, Editor in Chief, *Parents*, *Real Simple* and *People Magazine*

"When you find yourself not knowing where to turn, *Out* is like sitting down with a trusted friend. This is the go to resource for any parent supporting their LGBTQIA+ kid through the coming out process."

—Stacy London, TV personality, CEO State of Menopause

"The book's conversational style truly translates complex themes into easily digestible topics that are sure to amplify support for all LGBTQIA+ kids! A must read for supporting today's LGBTQIA+ youth."

—Nick Grant, PhD, ABPP, President, GLMA: Health Professionals Advancing LGBTQ+ Equality

"*Out* is a comprehensive guide for parents who want to be there for their LGBTQIA+ kid's journey in the most supportive way possible. If you have questions, fears, or concerns, this book is an incredible resource to educate yourself, so you can respond to your child with love."

—Kristin Johansen, actress, activist and mom to trans teen actor Isaiah Stannard

"The best thing about this book is that you don't have to know anything before you pick it up—all you need to do is start on page one. It's not technical, it's deeply personal, in a way that can only come from years of working with LGBTQ+ youth and their families."

—Dr. Laura Erickson-Schroth, Editor of Trans Bodies, Trans Selves, Chief Medical Officer at the Jed Foundation

"A powerful, intelligent, and empathetic book that guides parents and professionals in supporting LGBTQIA+ kids through the coming out process. *Out* addresses many of the fears and anxieties parents of LGBTQIA+ children face in a kind and compassionate manner."

—Dr. Dustin Nowaskie, Founder & President OutCare Health

OUT

of *related interest*

Coming Out Stories
Personal Experiences of Coming Out from Across the LGBTQ+ Spectrum
Edited by Emma Goswell and Sam Walker
ISBN 978 1 78775 495 9
eISBN 978 1 78775 496 6

Helping Your Transgender Teen 2nd Edition
A Guide for Parents
Irwin Krieger
ISBN 978 1 78592 801 7
eISBN 978 1 78450 819 7

Becoming an Ally to the Gender-Expansive Child
A Guide for Parents and Carers
Anna Bianchi
ISBN 978 1 78592 051 6
eISBN 978 178450 305 5

Beyond Pronouns
The Essential Guide for Parents of Trans Children
Tammy Plunkett
Foreword by Mitchell Plunkett
ISBN 978 1 83997 114 3
eISBN 978 1 83997 113 6

Out

A Parent's Guide to Supporting
Your LGBTQIA+ Kid Through
Coming Out and Beyond

John Sovec, LMFT

Jessica Kingsley Publishers
London and Philadelphia

First published in Great Britain in 2023 by Jessica Kingsley Publishers
An imprint of John Murray Press

1

Copyright © John Sovec, LMFT 2023

A CIP catalogue record for this title is available from the British
Library and the Library of Congress

ISBN 978 1 83997 424 3
eISBN 978 1 83997 425 0

Printed and bound in the United States by
Integrated Books International

Jessica Kingsley Publishers' policy is to use papers that are natural,
renewable and recyclable products and made from wood grown
in sustainable forests. The logging and manufacturing processes
are expected to conform to the environmental regulations
of the country of origin.

Jessica Kingsley Publishers
Carmelite House
50 Victoria Embankment
London EC4Y 0DZ

www.jkp.com

John Murray Press
Part of Hodder & Stoughton Limited
An Hachette UK Company

Contents

Contents

Welcome!

My guess is that if you are picking up this book, either your kid has come out to you or you suspect that they may be coming out to you in the future. Congratulations!! You are already an affirming and, in my eyes, cool parent by joining me on these pages to discover the most powerful ways that you can support your newly minted, emotionally vulnerable, slightly awkward, possibly insecure, and unquestionably amazing LGBTQIA+ kid.

Maybe the best way to begin this journey together is for us to take a moment to introduce ourselves. Hi! My name is John Sovec, LMFT, pronouns he/him, and I am an openly queer therapist who specializes in working with LGBTQIA+ youth and their families during the coming-out process. I speak all around the world on how we all need to come together and do the work to create affirming spaces for all LGBTQIA+ people but especially for LGBTQIA+ kids. I have been doing this work for many years now and find deep personal satisfaction in being a source of support for families and kids as they traverse the journey of coming out.

When I was a kid, the thought of being an openly gay person, having a powerful and productive life, and building a family all seemed impossible. There was little or no representation of my community in film, television, books, or media and the few times I saw people like me they were the neutered side-kick dropped in for comic relief. Or the other popular trope of the day was that LGBTQIA+ people were represented as perverse, dangerous, hyper-sexual, and salacious. It wasn't very affirming for an eight-year-old watching television with his parents and knowing deep inside that somehow those images I was witnessing were supposed to represent my future. Talk about feeling confused, marginalized, and insecure.

And yes, I knew I was gay at eight. Maybe not a complete picture of what being gay meant but a very deep internal knowledge that a core part of me was different from the other kids I hung out with. Most of my friends were gossiping about kids of the opposite sex, with all the other boys getting all giggly, squirmy, and weird toward the girls in our school. Meanwhile, my first crush as a kid was my friend Claude, a beautiful, wild spirit who made me feel a certain sensation of longing and just wanting to be around him. Later in junior high, as the hormone-induced maelstrom of puberty began to set in, those awkward attractions turned into desire and craving to be in a relationship with a guy. Any guy! It was a lot!

That was probably the moment when I could have used some help from a well-meaning teacher, an LGBTQIA+-affirming thera-pist, or even a best gay friend to work things through with. Initially, I did not even know how I would tell my parents and did not view them as a source of support for my budding queer identity. At that time, when I was drowning in the confusion and mixed messages of my body, my mind, and the world around me, most of those resources weren't available to me, and maybe your LGBTQIA+ kid is going through something similar. Although there are a lot more resources available for kids coming out today, accessing them can feel embarrassing and there can still be a certain awkwardness that accompanies the initial moments of realizing you are different from your peers.

And that is how you and I ended up here. I want to be that person who has lived experience and professional training to help you and your family through the coming-out process. I will be your steadfast and trustworthy LGBTQIA+ coming out guide and together we will trek into this unknown wilderness to give you the tools and understanding to be an amazing, affirming, and loving parent for your LGBTQIA+ child.

If you find yourself with immediate questions, fears, and concerns about your LGBTQIA+ kid, I suggest skipping ahead to the LGBTQIA+ FAQs and SOS Help Guide and the Resources section at the end of this book. Once some of those initial fears have been addressed, come back here and we can continue on together.

This book is designed to be an informative guide but also a catalyst for self-reflection on your part. Coming out is an amazing, powerful process and even though your LGBTQIA+ child's identity may be the stone dropped in the middle of the pond, the ripples and waves will affect the entire family. Rather than feeling fearful about these changes, I invite you, as you read through this book, to explore your own notions of sexual orientation and gender identity. Reflect on the messages you received from your family, friends, school, community at large, school, and religious community, noticing how they may not entirely reflect the reality of the world you live in today. If you are willing to take the plunge, this book will not only assist you in supporting your LGBTQIA+ child as they come out but also push your personal boundaries and allow you to grow and expand as well.

Buckle up, it's going to be a bumpy ride!

CHAPTER 1

The Words You Need

Being a parent who is suddenly thrust into the LGBTQIA+ world and expected to navigate the nuanced and ever-evolving landscape of sexual and gender expression and identity can be confusing, intimidating, and overwhelming. With all kinds of new words, definitions, and phrases that you're supposed to magically process and incorporate into your communications, it can feel like being thrown into the deep end of the pool without swimming lessons or floaties. Even the most open, affirming, and well-meaning parents I work with often feel awkward and adrift trying to get their heads around the "right" way to interact with their newly out or questioning LGBTQIA+ kid. They want to be respectful, correct, and up to date with all the information that's out there, but find the process of retraining their minds to adjust old speech patterns, examine lifelong culturally ingrained ideas about sex and gender and the way they're expressed, as well as letting go of preconceptions and expectations about the way they thought their kid would turn out, to be more work than they ever imagined.

As a jumping off point, let's pause for a moment, take a breath, and together develop a vocabulary that we can use throughout this book. I hope that in your interactions with your community, your family, and your kid, these definitions will make you feel more comfortable and confident. This moment of creating a shared vocabulary is the first step to building a strong foundation in your affirming approach to supporting your LGBTQIA+ child.

Let's begin with some of the most basic definitions and understanding regarding sex and gender. Please be aware that, even though I describe them as basic, they can often feel much more complex, provocative, and challenging to the core concepts that you were taught growing up and have taken for granted your whole life. I encourage you to take some time with these concepts and notice which ones cause you some anxiety because they push against your preconceived notions of gender and sex, or right and wrong. These are probably the concepts that are going to require the most work and awareness on your part, and you may want to sit for a moment and take a deeper dive. Even when it feels a little uncomfortable, knowledge can assist you in pushing past your anxiety, and reflection will help you to acknowledge your own biases.

The five terms and concepts we are going to define, discuss, and develop a greater understanding of are:

- Biological sex
- Gender
- Gender identity
- Gender expression
- Sexual orientation.

These terms and concepts are often thrown about carelessly, without a deeper understanding, and are often thought of as interchangeable; grasping the differences, nuances, and distinctions between them is vital for you as a parent to understand, protect, and support your LGBTQIA+ child on their journey of growth and development.

Biological sex

The first concept we will look at is biological sex. You're probably suddenly flashing back to your high school biology class but don't panic, there is no test at the end of this section. This is an easy place to start the conversation. Biological sex is simply the biological, genetic, or physical characteristics that define males and females. It's important to understand that this is solely based on an individual's biology, physical appearance, and chromosomes, and not anything else about your child. It's also important to understand that our biological sex is often assigned by well-meaning doctors who simply look at the external sex organs of a newborn as a means of identifying their sex and then add this information to their birth certificate.

That word, assigned, is an important concept to integrate into your awareness of biological sex in that myriad assumptions are made about sex simply based on a casual examination of external genitalia, not only at birth but throughout most of the life cycle. Unfortunately, the reality of biological sex is much more complex than two X chromosomes equal a girl with a vagina, and an X and a Y chromosome equal a boy with a penis. But more on that later. This may seem confusing at first but as we talk more about a transgender child's journey, this concept of "assignment" is the vital fact for you to understand.

Gender

Now, let's look at the word gender. Gender is the collection of social, psychological, and emotional traits often created by societal expectations to define what is masculine or feminine, male and female. Pause, take a breath, and read that sentence again. Gender is the collection of social, psychological, and emotional traits often created by societal expectations to define what is masculine or feminine, male and female. The operative word here is society's *expectations*.

Gender, as we experience it, is defined by the society where it's happening. A quick example of how society creates gender constructs is simply the phrase, "little girls wear pink." Another phrase that is common with gender identification is, "boys don't cry." These simple phrases are an example of how we as a society have decided what makes a girl and what makes a boy. These social constructs are omnipresent and overwhelming, with constant messaging through film, television, social media, and especially advertising that bombards you and your kid every day, promoting and cementing expected cultural gender roles and wielding enormous influence. Ask yourself what happens when a young girl acts in a way that seems more like the way a young boy would act. She's often teased and called a tomboy. When a young boy acts in a way that seems more like the way a young girl is expected to act, he's called a sissy or told to "man up." These labels can be applied as early as two, three, and four years of age, and the lasting impact of those labels and perceptions has enormous influence on a child's journey of self-understanding and acceptance. In fact, we begin gendering children in utero, through "gender reveal" parties. We are eager, at the first opportunity, to begin to see children through gendered glasses.

It's also important to understand the influence of varied cultural stories on our personal understanding of how gender works. Each culture creates standards about the way people should behave based on their gender. In some cultures, it's perfectly okay for men to walk arm in arm down a street and in others it's okay for them to kiss a greeting hello and goodbye. This is not seen as an expression of gay or same-sex attraction, it is simply a cultural construct of how men interact with each other. Cultural standards about gender are also commonly influenced by religious belief systems and traditions with well-defined roles of how a male or a female is expected to act within that religion's community. Perhaps this is a moment for you to contemplate how your understanding of what gender looks like is influenced by the way you were raised, by the gender roles you learned from your parents and other adults you were close to when you were a child, by religious influences in your upbringing, and by your community at large.

The thing I find most parents have difficulty with is that they've never really had to reflect on the question of gender. It's one of the core concepts that is drilled into us literally from the moment we're born. It's the first thing that is noted about us when we come into the world. It's how we are organized and categorized from the way we're clothed, to the toys we're given, to the way we are taught and guided in school. Boys in this line; girls in that line (usually in that order). Boys use this restroom; girls use that restroom. Boys play on this sports team; girls play on that sports team. A male teacher is Mr.; a female teacher is Ms. Boys have girlfriends; girls have boyfriends. Our binary one-or-the-other concept of gender is part of the bedrock of a world view that is drilled into us from the moment we begin to understand the world around us. Most of us never have much reason to question or examine that concept besides the vague knowledge that there are trans people out there, or people who don't want to be considered one gender or the other, but until we're confronted with someone we love, someone like our own kid, who is questioning or challenging their gender assignment, or acting in ways that are contrary to traditional gender roles, it's not something most of us confront. In fact, because of its place as a core concept in our world view, most people actively avoid examining it, whether consciously or not, because that fear of being a sissy or a tomboy taught us at a very young age about the danger of rocking the gender boat.

As a parent, it's important to understand that your kid, whether they are LGBTQIA+ or not, may be contemplating what gender means to them and how it influences their experience at school, with friends and peers, in interactions with their family, or in how they see themselves versus how others see them as they walk around the streets of your town. It's important to understand how these questions of gender are influencing your child and to be willing to look at how examining and shifting your view of gender might allow you to be a better source of support, safety, and affirmation for your kid.

Gender identity

Next up is gender identity. Just as gender is an external expression of how society and culture dictate the rules of what it means to be male or female, gender identity is a personal expression of how we express that gender to the world. Gender identity is a person's deeply held internal sense of being male, female, some of both, or maybe even neither. Where gender is created by society, an external factor, gender identity is a very deep personal internal feeling about who we are and how we interact with the world around us. Our feelings about our gender identity can show up at a very young age, sometimes as young as two or three. Many kids are also aware of a lot of pressure to fit in and identify as their assigned birth sex. This can have a significant impact on their physical, emotional, and mental wellness if their gender identity is at odds with society's expectations of their assigned birth sex. In other words, gender identity is something we intuitively know about ourselves. It cannot be seen, regardless of how we were assigned at birth. Someone's gender identity is only known if it is shared.

If you look at a kid who may be questioning their gender iden-tity or identifying differently from their biological assigned sex, think how difficult that journey might be, how much hostility, rejection, even violence they may face for outwardly challenging that most basic core concept we've all had drilled into us. Imagine the conflict they must feel between the weight of expectation that has been placed on them by family, school, and peers based on their assigned biological sex and its accompanying external expression that may not agree with who they are on the inside. It's important to understand the pain, struggle, and shame that is often inherent in this journey and to be present with it, even though it may be challenging and confusing for you as a parent, especially when you might be the target or outlet for your child's anger, frustration, and confusion. The best advice I can offer as your kid begins to openly express their gender identity is to simply listen and meet them where they are at without judgment.

Gender expression

Now, let's take a look at gender expression. Gender expression is how your child grabs hold of their gender identity and then presents themselves to the world. It is the way in which a person communicates their gender identity, that internal sense of who they are, to others by external means. This can be through the clothing they wear, their makeup, hairstyles, personal mannerisms, speech patterns, and style of social interactions. This is also where teens explore the use of names and pronouns that are more authentic to their identity.

Another way to look at this is that gender expression is simply how we choose to appear to the world in alignment with our gender identity. Making a choice to wear a collared shirt and tie, to wear a dress, to wear high heels, to wear combat boots; all of these are embracing or pushing against culturally contrived stories of gender expression.

What's vital to understand with kids and their gender expression is that this may change from year to year, month to month, and day to day. This is a journey, a search for creating agreement between gender identity, that internal sense of self, and gender expression, how they appear in their world. I often advise parents, especially those with teenagers, not to get caught up in the day-to-day ebbs and flows of their kid's exploration and experimentation, but instead, to be supportive of their long-term journey. And it might also be an interesting challenge for you as a parent to push the boundaries of your own gender expression in the world.

Sexual orientation

Finally, we come to the question of sexual orientation. It's important to understand that sexual orientation is completely separate from gender identity and gender expression. Often these phrases are confused or convoluted in people's conversations and in the media. We need to encourage awareness, understanding, and education about the fact that sexual orientation is completely separate from gender identity and expression.

So, what is sexual orientation? It is simply the combination of characteristics in others, including but not limited to gender and sex, that a person is attracted to emotionally, romantically, intellectually, physically, or sexually. In essence, our sexual orientation defines the targets of our sexual feelings toward other people. Sexual orientation may be driven by a person's attraction to a certain gender, or it may have fluidity that is not confined to a particular sex or gender expression at all. This is often a difficult concept for parents to grasp and accept because, again, it challenges that first core binary lesson, boy or girl, and later, straight or gay, one or the other. When addressing sexual orientation, it is also vital to understand that transgender and non-binary people can be gay, straight, bisexual, pansexual, or another unique attraction. They may also be asexual or demisexual. This may feel confusing but it is important to understand that a person's gender identity exists independently of a person's sexual orientation. A trans female may be attracted to other females, males, transgender people of any gender, and/or non-binary people. The same is true for a transgender male. The important thing to understand is that each individual is unique and will have their own unique combination and interplay of gender identity and sexual orientation. Letting go of preconceived ideas about this or that and one or the other will help you open your mind so you can listen to and understand what your kid is telling you about their individual blend of gender and sexual orientation.

Even parents who think of themselves as open and accepting may find themselves challenged by LGBTQIA+ kids whose sexual orientation doesn't fit into one of the familiar labels that we use to categorize people. It is also important to understand that a person's sexual orientation may evolve and develop over time. The reality, whether we as a society are ready to accept it or not, is that far more people than our society is comfortable acknowledging fall somewhere in the middle of this attraction binary that we have grown up with. As with all these terms and concepts, the best thing you as a parent can do for your kid, as they work out who they are and who and what they want, is to educate yourself so you can be present without judgment and better support and protect them on their journey.

Many years ago, as I was beginning my work with LGBTQIA+ kids and families, a colleague shared a simple idea that crystalized the difference between sexual orientation and gender identity for me, and I have been sharing it with parents and kids ever since. The difference between sexual orientation and gender identity is simply this: sexual orientation is who we go to bed with, and gender identity is who we go to bed as. Get your head around this concept and you'll have a huge head start compared with the rest of the adults in your kid's life. And who knows? Your kid might even think you're cool.

Now that you've been introduced to the core terms and concepts you need to navigate the LGBTQIA+ journey you'll be taking with your kid, it's important to return to these definitions over and over so that they override your old cultural programming and become your new normal. I also encourage you, as a parent, to be gentle with yourself during this process of learning and to be okay with making mistakes. For many kids, the mere fact that their parent is committed to learning, growing, and embracing these adjustments, even if they're not perfect starting at day one, is enough to carry a family through the challenges and rigors of their kid's coming out journey.

Questions for contemplation

1. How does your upbringing, including family stories, culture, and religion, influence how you view gender? Sexual orientation?
2. How does popular media (film, television, books, social media) influence your perceptions of gender? Sexual orientation?
3. How do you express your gender identity each day?
4. What are some of the assumptions you make daily based on someone's external appearance?
5. What is it like each day for your kid as they are struggling to express their gender identity to the world? How can you support that journey of discovery?

CHAPTER 2

More Words You Need

In the last chapter, we began establishing a new vocabulary to help us better communicate about concepts like gender, gender expression, and gender identity. We've also defined accurate terms and descriptions for sexual orientation. But there's additional vocabulary that defines LGBTQIA+ identity which is also important to learn and understand. If you've done a search about sexual orientation or gender identity on the internet, you may have encountered long acronyms with intimidating strings of letters, numbers, and symbols bundled together, like LGBT2QIASAGPDDSM*, and maybe even longer ones than that. Trying to understand and remember all these terms and their often-evolving nuances can feel daunting, discouraging, and overwhelming to even the most well-intentioned and affirming parent.

Let's rein in the panic and begin with a preliminary array of letters to give you the basic knowledge you need to initiate a dialogue between you and your kid. This short list is certainly not all-encompassing of the vast array of terms used in our community, but it should get you headed in the right direction and hopefully deepen your curiosity to explore further. One of the more commonly used acronyms that you have probably seen, and the one we will use in this book, is LGBTQIA+. There are small internal variations of this collection of letters, and they only represent a fraction of our rainbow community but once again, let's start small and build as we go.

L: Lesbian

The first letter in the LGBTQIA+ acronym is L, which stands for lesbian. Used as a descriptor for sexual orientation, which is who you have sex with and experience sexual attraction for, lesbian describes a female who has emotional, romantic, intellectual, sexual, physical attraction or behavior with another female. Or, as my clients sometimes like to say, it's "girls who are into girls." Most females who identify as gay usually use the word lesbian to describe themselves for a very good reason. For many years, the word gay was used as a blanket term for the community, but over time and with shifting social and cultural diversity, many females found that their needs were not being met or addressed by the wider community. In response to these challenges, it became much more common for females to use the word lesbian as their most accurate self-definition. This movement allowed them to create an environment where their needs from a social, spiritual, community, medical, and mental health standpoint were being addressed in a more sustained and direct way. Like many of the terms we will discuss, age, heritage, and geography may impact what word a person uses to identify themselves. Older women seem more likely to use lesbian, while younger women may use gay or queer. Remember to follow the lead of your child when they use a word to identify themselves.

G: Gay

For a male, the identifier used most often is represented by the letter G in LGBTQIA+, which stands for gay. In this context, gay is the term used to describe a male who has emotional, romantic, intellectual, sexual, physical attraction or behavior with another male. The term gay is often used by men in the community as a way of identifying themselves to others. But as mentioned above, there are instances when lesbians and others may also refer to themselves as gay, using it as a blanket term to indicate same-sex/gender attraction and sexual orientation, so there is some fluidity to the definition of this term depending on the context and circumstances under which it is used. An important point I'd like to touch on in relation to the term gay is to encourage you to avoid identifying gay and lesbian people as "homosexuals." While this term has been around for over a century, it has not aged well due to its use by law enforcement and in negative political rhetoric targeting the LGBTQIA+ community. Historically, it has also had negative connotations and been used as a medical term to diagnose LGBTQIA+ people as suffering from a mental illness, and is pathologizing in its meaning. In this day and age, it is viewed as an outdated term and considered derogatory and offensive to many lesbian and gay people.

In both instances above, as well as those we have yet to discuss, these terms are not just used to describe who a person is attracted to sexually but also to encompass myriad varieties of attraction, including emotional, intellectual, romantic, and desire for companionship, some or all of which may or may not overlap in a person's experience of attraction. Often, if I tell someone that I'm gay, I can see the wheels turning in their mind and the immediate conclusion they draw is usually, "oh, he has sex with guys!" While that is accurate, boiling down an LGBTQIA+ person's sexual orientation and identity to a sex act is narrow and limiting. It ignores the profound impact that going against traditional cultural norms to discover, accept, and embrace a key part of themselves has on their identity. While sexual attractions are often the catalysts that lead to teens' initial realization that their sexual orientation falls somewhere in the LGBTQIA+ alphabet, I believe it is vital that parents of LGBTQIA+ teens look beyond those physical sexual attractions and become curious about the other facets of their teen's emerging identity as they begin to understand who they are and what they want. It can be a powerful shift when you can interact with LGBTQIA+ people of all ages and not just focus on who they have sex with, but rather strive to acknowledge and understand the uniqueness of their journey and its role in shaping who they are.

B: Bisexual

The next letter in the LGBTQIA+ alphabet is B, which stands for bisexual. In terms of its definition and the place bisexual people occupy in the LGBTQIA+ community, this definition is probably the most nuanced and contentious of any of the terms we'll discuss. Traditionally, the term bisexual described a male or female who has emotional, romantic, intellectual, sexual, physical attraction or behavior for both men and women; hence the "bi" prefix, referencing two genders to which an individual might be attracted. While this term is still widely used by people to describe their sexuality, our society's evolving understanding of gender and the resulting shift away from a strictly binary model is leading many to rethink their use of this term to describe themselves and others. At this point in time, the term bisexual is often used to indicate people who have attraction to two *or more* genders.

Unfortunately, many people who come out as bisexual are initially met with skepticism and even derision, and, most disappointingly, from others in the LGBTQIA+ community. This is less common for females who come out and identify as bisexual. Although they may be marginalized to some extent, there is often more support and acceptance from their peers, parents, and the community around them. For males, there is often a pernicious assumption, frequently aimed at those who have recently come out as bisexual, that they're really just gay but too afraid to admit it, as if saying they're bisexual is a way of easing into their same-sex attraction without fully committing. They often find themselves the butt of jokes and feeling marginalized because people don't accept the idea of someone not being one thing or the other.

As we discussed in the last chapter, that binary concept of male or female, masculine or feminine, straight or gay, one thing or the other is so deeply ingrained in us that even those who have had to endure the difficulty of coming out and acknowledging their own "otherness" within our culture struggle, and often fail to acknowledge and accept the reality of bisexual people. The unfortunate result is that bisexual people can end up feeling rejected and isolated and may struggle to establish and maintain healthy romantic relationships.

For this reason, it is so important to meet your kid where they are when they identify their sexual orientation. Make the effort to learn, understand, and use the words and terms they use to describe themselves. As we have discussed, sexual orientation can be fluid. It can evolve and change over time. Your job as a parent is to support and affirm your kid's journey. And that may mean overcoming deeply ingrained assumptions on your part. It may also mean accepting a future evolution of your kid's identity.

An important thing to understand about anyone who is bisexual, irrespective of their gender, is that while the term bisexual indicates that an individual's attraction can exist for multiple genders, it does not necessarily mean that all bisexual people are equally attracted to all genders. Oftentimes, a bisexual person's attraction to one gender may be more dominant and compelling, while their attraction to another gender only surfaces occasionally or intermittently. Also, it is important to understand that a bisexual person's attraction to multiple genders does not mean they can't or won't engage in a monogamous relationship with a partner, irrespective of their partner's gender.

Now, as I mentioned earlier, our society's views and understanding of gender are evolving, and the traditional binary concept that people are strictly either male or female is no longer accepted as the full story of gender and its relationship to attraction. As I mentioned, while some kids may identify as bisexual, a newer term that's gaining traction is pansexual, which is the emotional, romantic, intellectual, sexual, physical attraction or behavior with another person regardless of their gender. I know you may be scratching your head, asking yourself, "what's the difference?" I get it. It's a nuanced distinction, but an important one.

Pansexuality is the potential for attraction to the full range of genders, gender identities, and gender expressions that an individual may encounter. In essence, pansexual people's attraction is not dependent on or constrained by gender. This differs from bisexuality, which generally indicates the attraction to two *or more* genders, but not necessarily all, which means that a bisexual person's attraction may be constrained by gender, where a pansexual person's attraction is not. As with bisexual people, pansexual people may not necessarily be attracted to all genders equally at all times and may or may not pursue monogamous relationships with partners of any gender.

As always, in defining these terms I'm sharing the general understanding that exists at the present time. Individual people may understand and interpret these terms differently now or in the future, which is why understanding that your kid's identity is an evolving journey rather than a static destination is so important. Ultimately, your job as a parent and ally is to communicate openly and often so that you know what term or terms your kid identifies with, learn what they mean to society and to your kid, then love and support them in that identity.

I know that was a lot, but this is a very important concept to embrace. May I suggest you reread that last section and then maybe take a break and sort through any confusion, feelings, or fears that might be rising up. As I keep joking, there will not be a quiz at the end of the chapter, but this information may be new for many of you and push against the narratives that you have grown up with and the lens through which you view the world.

T: Transgender

The next term in our new vocabulary is represented by the letter T, which stands for transgender. We will spend more time exploring and learning what it means to be transgender a little further into this book, but for now it is important to understand some differences between this term and the others that we've discussed in this chapter. The other terms we've defined so far all pertain to a person's sexual orientation, the part of a person's sexual identity that determines the characteristics of the people they're attracted to. Transgender is not a sexual orientation. The simplest definition of transgender is an individual whose gender identity, that's their internal conviction and sense of their gender, differs from the biological sex they were assigned at birth. Transgender people can be lesbian, gay, bisexual, pansexual, or any other term that may accurately describe their sexual orientation. As we noted earlier, gender, gender identity, gender expression, and biological sex are all unique components that contribute to an individual's identity and differ from sexual orientation.

Q: Queer

The next letter in the LGBTQIA+ acronym is Q, which actually stands for two terms. The first of these is queer. Many people react with discomfort to the term queer because they know it as a derogatory word, a slur used to insult and degrade the LGBTQIA+ community.

For most of the last hundred years that was the case, but now many LGBTQIA+ people are taking this word back and using it as a descriptor of empowerment. It is difficult to assign a strict definition to this term, and it is probably best not to do so, since it is used to encompass a wide variety of people, characteristics, behaviors, and communities. Queer is commonly used as an umbrella term to describe someone who does not conform to rigid or traditional notions of gender and sexuality. It may be used by people who identify as any of the terms we've already discussed, but also by those for whom the other common terms used to describe gender and sexual orientation don't feel like a good fit. It also frequently has sociopolitical connotations and is favored by activists. Queer can be an umbrella term used by anyone who is LGBTQIA+ and can convey a sense of orientation, gender, as well as a connection to community. Please be aware that while the word "queer" used within the community is generally viewed as positive, some LGBTQIA+ people (especially LGBTQIA+ elders) still find it a painful and uncomfortable word due to its discriminatory history. I personally identify as queer, although you may hear me switch back and forth between queer and gay. For me, queer embraces the many aspects of who I am and recognizes the power that I choose to take as an out and proud member of my community.

Q: Questioning

The second term represented by Q is questioning, which describes what can be a frighteningly vulnerable time in an LGBTQIA+ kid's life. Questioning refers to an exploratory, developmental, and experimental phase when LGBTQIA+ kids realize that they are not or might not be "straight" or "cis" and begin a deep dive into defining their sexual orientation and/or gender identity. Questioning can happen at any time in a person's life, but it can be particularly

difficult for teens due to the scrutiny, self-consciousness, and volatile pressurized social environments they often face. During this
time, your kid may be exploring, discovering, or unsure about their
sexual orientation or gender identity. Questioning does not always
equate to confusion. Rather, it is a powerful developmental stage
in an adolescent's life in which they pursue self-awareness and
begin to take control of their identity. It is interesting to note that
although we are defining this questioning phase within the context
of LGBTQIA+ kids, questioning one's sexual orientation or gender
identity is a normal part of human development, regardless of one's
ultimate sexual orientation or gender identity.

If your teen is questioning, your job as a parent and ally is to
be supportive and provide a safe environment where they can talk
about what they're feeling and experiencing without the fear they
will be rejected or disappoint you. As hard as it can be for a parent
to witness this uncertainty in their child, it is important not to
jump into "fix-it" mode where, with the best intentions, you push
your kid to "figure things out" and come to a conclusion. These
discoveries must happen in their own time, and while your natural
parental instinct may be to lead and guide your kid, on this journey,
you're the passenger, not the driver.

I: Intersex

An intersex person is one whose biological sex does not correspond
with conventional expectations of male or female anatomy or
genetics. These biological and chromosomal variations are far more
common than you may think, as much as 2 percent of the general
population, and often remain undetected until later in a person's
life. There is a variety of circumstances and characteristics that may
result in a person being intersex. These may include having genitals
that fall outside the male or female categories, perhaps even having

both ovarian and testicular tissues. In other instances, there may be combinations of chromosomes that differ from the range of XX, female chromosomes, and XY, male chromosomes, that other people might exhibit, such as XXY.

If a child's genitals differ from what their doctor may expect from a male or female at birth, their intersex identity is often discovered at a young age. For others, especially when the differences are not reflected in easily observable anatomy, but rather in their chromosomal makeup, their intersex identity may not become known until puberty, later in life, or, in some cases, intersex people might live their entire lives without discovering their bodies' unique coding. As with those who are transgender, intersex is not an indicator of sexual orientation. Intersex people can be any sexual orientation and can identify with any gender identity or expression.

If you have a child who is intersex, the best thing you can do is to educate yourself and your child about what it means to be intersex. As with any aspect of their identity, support them and love them for who they are. It's also a good idea to ensure that you have informed medical support and access to a doctor who understands the potential health implications for intersex people, as they may experience health complications as a result of being intersex. Most importantly, seek support from other parents with children who are intersex and work to provide your child with opportunities to connect with other intersex children.

A: Asexual

The final letter I want to cover in our LGBTQIA+ alphabet is A, which, like Q, represents two separate terms. The first of these is asexual. While the experience of each asexual person is unique, in general, an asexual person is someone who experiences little to no physical sexual attraction, has little or no desire to engage in sexual activity with other people, and experiences little to no emotional satisfaction or pleasure from doing so. It is important not to pathologize this or make it a deficit-based story. Asexuality is different from celibacy, which is abstinence from sex by personal choice or conviction but does not denote the absence of sexual attraction or desire. Instead, an asexual person has limited or no physical or sexual arousal toward other people. The expression and experience of asexuality from person to person is wide-ranging and encompasses many variables and nuances. Asexual people's feelings about physical sexual contact may range from indifference to disgust. However, being asexual does not mean that an individual cannot or will not have deep, fulfilling, committed emotional and/or romantic relationships with others. As a result, if you are the parent of an asexual kid, sometimes referred to as ace, it is vital that you support them by reinforcing that they are not broken, sick, incomplete, deficient, or destined to spend their lives alone, especially as they are surrounded by the raging hormones and sexual awakenings of their peers with whom they will invariably be comparing themselves.

A: Ally

The second term represented by A is ally. An ally is a person just like you, a parent, a family member, a teacher, a coach, a friend, anyone who is present, educated, loving, affirming, and supportive of LGBTQIA+ people as they travel through their coming-out process and their lives.

The definitions I am sharing here are just the tip of a deep and expressive vocabulary and it is important to understand that these terms will shift and change over time as they become even more nuanced. Remember too, that these definitions are just that, definitions. They are not the embodiment of that very real flesh and blood child who has just come out to you and, ultimately, they are the most powerful and authentic expression of any of these terms and identities.

So, now you can congratulate yourself on your newfound understanding of the most common terms and characteristics that define the LGBTQIA+ community. And yes, your brain may be on the verge of exploding right now and that's okay. You don't need to master everything on day one. Just as the coming-out process can take time, the journey of learning about your kid's LGBTQIA+ experience is also a journey that takes time, effort, and patience. As a parent, it is important to give yourself space to learn and permission to make mistakes, and to commit to being curious and open to everything that's out there.

Questions for contemplation

1. What are some of the assumptions you make every day about someone's sexual orientation?
2. How do you react inside your heart and mind when you see media representation of a sexual orientation that is not yours?
3. How do you imagine it might feel for your kid when their self-definition doesn't fall within the cis/heteronormative definitions?
4. How challenging is it for you to embrace the myriad possibilities of sexual orientation and gender identity that are being presented on these pages?
5. Are there terms defined here that you would like to investigate further either for yourself or your child's well-being?

CHAPTER 3

Coming Out

It's a Process

A s a parent, one of your strongest natural instincts is to protect
your kid. When your kid comes out, particularly if you're a
parent for whom your kid's LGBTQIA+ identity is a surprise, you're
suddenly faced with a new and very real situation fraught with
complexity, nuance, and perceived threats that may kick your
mama/papa bear instincts into high gear. While that is a perfectly
natural response, your kid's LGBTQIA+ identity is not a threat from
which they need to be protected. Letting those reactive protective
instincts overtake your ability to think and act rationally with
intention and love can be problematic and even dangerous at this
emotionally charged moment when your relationship with your kid
is particularly vulnerable.

The majority of parents in our society are straight cisgender
people. Even if you came of age with *Will and Grace*, *Pose*, and *Queer
Eye*, grasping what it means to realize you're different, potentially
from a very early age, acknowledge it, then find the courage and
resolve to come out is something most parents haven't experienced
for themselves. As you now know from the last few chapters, there
is an extensive vocabulary and complex language for describing

and talking about LGBTQIA+ life and people. By the time your kid comes out to you, they have probably spent a lot of time on the internet and talking with friends to find the right words to describe who they are. This means you as the parent have a lot of catching up to do to educate yourself and that can leave you feeling stressed, unprepared, frightened, and overwhelmed. The most important thing you can do as you're confronted with these charged feelings is to slow down, take a breath, reassure your kid that you love them, that you are here for them, that you may make mistakes, and that you will learn and grow together on this journey.

One scenario that is common when a kid first comes out in a supportive household is that there is an initial flood of love, attention, and support. Then, once those initial scenes of revelation and response play out, everyone moves on and nobody ever talks about it again. Not the parents, not the LGBTQIA+ kid, nobody. This may not necessarily be done out of fear or discomfort, but rather because of a lack of understanding that coming out is an ongoing process that doesn't end at the moment when your kid comes out to *you*. One of the first things I encourage you to understand is that by its very nature and description, coming out is an ongoing, lifelong process. It's not a one-and-done experience, like getting your driver's license, where you come out, get your official queer membership card, and then go about your out and proud life. Coming out is a continuous and evolving experience that occurs every time an LGBTQIA+ person meets another human, applies for a job, goes into a restaurant, answers a phone call. Every human interaction an LGBTQIA+ person has is infused with an element of coming out, even if there isn't an explicit verbal communication of a person's LGBTQIA+ identity. There is always the element of navigating interactions where LGBTQIA+ people assess whether others perceive their identity, identify whether that perception could be an ally or a threat, and plan their actions and potential contingencies accordingly.

For many LGBTQIA+ people, this internal process starts early in childhood, becoming so habitual and ingrained that they don't consciously realize it's happening. It takes a lot of emotional energy to maintain that level of processing and vigilance and, eventually, it can take its toll on a person's emotional and mental health. This is something I encourage you, as the parent of an LGBTQIA+ kid, to keep in the forefront of your mind as you work to support your kid on their coming-out journey. This is where it can be especially helpful for parents to get educated and find a support network, whether it is by joining your local LGBTQIA+ parent support group, or a step as simple as reading this book. What is important is that you do everything you can to understand the journey that your LGBTQIA+ child is on and strive to provide meaningful support.

Another concept that is important for parents of LGBTQIA+ kids to grasp is that coming out is just one step in your kid's exploration of their sexual orientation and gender identity. And while it may be the first step for you as a supporter of your kid's journey, that step is often the culmination of years of questioning, self-examination, agonizing, exploring, acknowledging, and, finally, communicating.

As a therapist who specializes in working with LGBTQIA+ kids, I often find myself in situations where I am the first person they come out to. It is a profound moment to witness their realization as they say out loud for the first time to another person, "I'm gay," "I'm trans," "I'm bi," or even just, "I'm not straight." But even once these words are spoken out loud, it is just one step in a multi-faceted developmental process that is ongoing and will continue throughout their life. This developmental process touches every aspect of an LGBTQIA+ kid's life, including learning how being out influences their school experience and their social interactions, exploring what it means to date and build relationships as an out person, confronting questions of religion and spiritual belief systems, and building an LGBTQIA+ community of support.

I've talked a lot about this developmental process that LGBT-QIA+ kids experience. While each kid's journey is unique, there is a pattern that seems to exist in the path kids follow on their way to coming out. If you've looked around online, you've probably found an array of coming-out models developed by researchers over the years. In my work with kids throughout my career, I've examined, applied, and analyzed many of those models in an effort to educate myself and understand the way our society defines the LGBTQIA+ experience, and particularly coming out. Not surprisingly, as our society's understanding of psychology, sexuality, identity, and gender has evolved, many of those models have become outdated and outmoded. In some cases, the models are helpful but are either too specific or too vague, sometimes missing or overemphasizing key developmental milestones and ultimately confusing rather than clarifying the coming-out journey. Through extensive research of the current scientific models, coupled with my own experiences with kids who are coming out and their families, I have worked to shape the insights I've gleaned into a parent-friendly explanation of the three phases most LGBTQIA+ kids experience as they come out.

The introspection phase

At a very young age, sometimes as young as three to five years old, LGBTQIA+ kids may begin noticing that they don't fit into the social constructs that they are witnessing their friends and peers integrating into effortlessly. These constructs include things like what makes a boy's toy versus what makes a girl's toy, the clothes that they are supposed to wear, the way they are supposed to interact with kids of the same or differing gender, their mannerisms, and even the inflections of their speech. These rules, dominated by traditional cisgender and heterocentric norms, can feel constraining, uncomfortable, and unnatural for young LGBTQIA+ kids, often without them understanding why or being able to articulate where the disconnect is. These social constructs are especially present in school systems and put a lot of pressure on LGBTQIA+ kids to be "normal" and conform to be like everyone else. For most kids, all they want to do is fit in and be liked by their peers. Not feeling able to do so from such a young age can be the beginning of a long and difficult spiral of internalized shame and alienation which, while not unique to LGBTQIA+ kids, is distressingly common.

This realization of "otherness," of not fitting into predetermined social constructs, often triggers what I identify as the introspection phase. For our purposes, introspection is that moment when LGBTQIA+ kids gain a sufficient level of self-awareness to start comparing themselves with their peers in an effort to understand how they fit in, or don't fit in, and begin questioning why that is. This is often the point at which they begin to question and explore the most basic foundations of what will become their sexual orientation and gender identity. They begin to notice that they are drawn to certain kids over others, gravitate toward certain genders over others, feel comfortable in some situations and uncomfortable in others. It is also the time when they begin to choose the parts of themselves that they believe they might need to mask and hide in order to fit in, and in some cases, maintain their personal safety. This is a time of deep internal examination, which can often externally manifest as anxiety and depression if the objects of their feelings of interest, affinity, and attraction are met with disapproval and disdain by their friends, family, and community.

The introspection phase is often when the seeds of "otherness" and internalized feelings of alienation take root. It is a point at which LGBTQIA+ kids will begin to make decisions about how much they are willing to risk to express their identity, pursue their interests, and carve out their place among their peers. It is also the time when LGBTQIA+ kids begin to realize that there are very real long-term consequences to those decisions. As I mentioned earlier, most kids simply want to fit in and be liked by their peers. These feelings of difference can also make many LGBTQIA+ kids feel less than, which can not only affect their mental health but also manifest in physical health challenges, behavior problems, and school performance issues.

Some of the feelings and inclinations LGBTQIA+ kids discover during the introspection phase can grow stronger over time and others may fade. It is usually at the point when puberty begins that things start to crystalize and the differences that LGBTQIA+ kids have been noticing and exploring start to take on a deeper meaning. As things like sexual sensations, body development/awareness, and attractions begin to manifest, the stakes in an LGBTQIA+ kid's development begin to feel exponentially higher and often result in overwhelm, anxiety, depression, and confusion.

It's common for parents to notice these symptoms without understanding their underlying source, which can lead to misunderstanding, frustration, and conflict at home, on top of the difficulties LGBTQIA+ kids are already facing. As a parent, if you suspect that your kid might be LGBTQIA+ and working to define their identity, it's important to consider the internal turmoil they are facing and how much work it takes for a kid to articulate to themselves, much less to their parents, what their identity is. Think about that the next time you're frustrated because they don't want to answer your questions about how their day went, and if they do, you get the ubiquitous "fine" in response. Your LGBTQIA+ kid may not even have the words yet to explain how difficult their day was or describe what's wrong.

Despite the difficulties that most LGBTQIA+ kids face articulating their feelings and experiences during the introspective phase, it is vital that you as a parent keep an open invitation for supportive communication so that your kid knows that there is a safe space to talk about these intense feelings when they are ready. And that is a key concept you need to pay attention to: *when they are ready*. Coming out is not something you can rush or force. It won't happen on your schedule. Instead, keep laying the groundwork of support and love that will let them know that they can talk to you when they have the words.

The identification phase

The moment when your kid may first be ready to start communicating and sharing about their LGBTQIA+ identity is what I refer to as the identification phase. This is that fragile moment when the feelings from those years of introspection, questioning, and exploring get so big that an LGBTQIA+ kid decides to start embracing and acknowledging their authentic identity to themselves, their family, their friends, and their community. It may manifest in a quiet, subtle way, or it may emerge with fanfare and a big splash. But one thing that I make a point of telling parents of LGBTQIA+ kids is that you will probably not be the first person your kid comes out to, and that is not something to be upset about. You are one of the most important people in your kid's life, whether they're willing to admit that or not. They are dependent on you, and your love and approval are irreplaceable. For your LGBTQIA+ kid, it may feel as if there is no greater risk than telling you who they really are, when it might end up costing them everything. Because of this, it is common for kids to come out to a close friend, a low-risk family member, a supportive teacher, or a therapist first as a way to test the waters and see what kind of reaction they might get. It is also a chance for them to rehearse how they want this high-stakes conversation to play out in a lower risk environment.

Some kids will piggyback on these trial conversations with a very conscientious, well-planned, and incredibly purposeful coming-out moment that gives them a sense of control over a challenging and anxiety-producing conversation. But with all these pressures and fears weighing on LGBTQIA+ kids as they contemplate coming out, it may be challenging for them to orchestrate the moment in the kind of graceful, well-thought-out manner worthy of an after-school special. Sometimes the coming-out conversation may be unplanned, unexpected, and explosive, triggered by an incident at school, a change in a kid's interpersonal relationships, or a breakup, or it might be presented in a confrontational manner during an argument. That's okay. In fact, it is often a moment of powerful growth when your kid communicates their LGBTQIA+ identity to you out loud for the first time, even if it happens amid strong or negative emotions. As awkward and challenging as this moment may feel for you, remember that this is a pinnacle moment in their personal development, and it is vital for them to have the space to express themselves, even if that expression is wrapped in anger or confrontation. Your kid is taking a critical step toward openly acknowledging and embracing their identity and living their life with authenticity.

The integration phase

The final phase in the coming-out process is what I describe as the integration phase. This is the point in an LGBTQIA+ kid's developmental process when all the tension and build-up to the moment of coming out has passed, their identity is no longer a secret to some or all of the people who really matter in their life, and they begin to integrate their authentic identity into their wider pursuits, activities, and relationships. It is the beginning of the ongoing experience of living an openly queer life with friends, family of choice, family of origin, in relationships, and a deeper, more personal connection to the LGBTQIA+ community. The integration phase will be different for every kid and will have unique moments and challenges depending on if they are coming out about their sexual orientation or their gender identity or both. For some it will be gradual and subtle, and may evolve over many years. For others, it may be a boisterous time of vibrant and assertive expression. For parents of LGBTQIA+ kids, this phase can be simultaneously exciting and stressful, a relief and an adjustment. It may feel as if your kid is becoming someone you don't recognize. They may start dressing and speaking differently. They may start spending time with new friends and cut ties with old ones. Relationships will alter, develop, and grow. They may exhibit new confidence and assertiveness that can be unsettling, but also exciting.

The changes that often surface during the integration phase are generally the result of your kid valuing and respecting their sexual orientation and gender identity, even if it is initially done clumsily and without finesse. It is a time when they can bring forward an identity that they may have been masking for years and make sense of their feelings, sensations, and attractions. Prior to coming out, most LGBTQIA+ kids have been struggling with the pressure of being different and not fitting into the social roles that a cisgender heterocentric society expects of them. Coming out and integrating their true self into their family, school, and community is an act of courage and rebellion that is often painful, frightening, and freeing all at the same time. But it is this act of courageous rebellion that opens the door for LGBTQIA+ kids to begin finding community, support, and relationships, and carving out a new place where they can fit in, rather than carving off pieces of themselves to fit into places where their authentic selves aren't welcome.

As a parent, you are an important and integral part of your kid's integration, and you'll need to find your own personal way to contribute to that supportive environment. You will need to confront your own fears, overcome your confusion, and find the path to affirming your kid's authentic self so that you can ensure your place as a partner and ally on their life journey. If you take a look online, you will find that a lot of kids have filmed their coming-out moment with one or both of their parents. One thing that many of these videos have in common is the anxiety and fear of rejection with which most kids approach the prospect of coming out to their parents. Even when they are confident that their parents are affirming and supportive of the wider LGBTQIA+ community, they are still likely to harbor deep core fears that their parents will reject them and withdraw their love.

The most supportive and powerful reaction you can have to your child coming out is to simply hug them tight and let them know that you love them. I am going to repeat that statement: The most supportive and powerful reaction you can have to your child coming out is to simply hug them tight and let them know that you love them. At this vulnerable moment, LGBTQIA+ kids need to be affirmed and reminded that they are a valuable and irreplaceable member of the family. And although you as a parent may be going through some big feelings of your own, loving affirmation toward your kid at this fragile moment will set a strong foundation for connection and communication as the coming-out process progresses.

Questions for contemplation

1. What messages, both overt and covert, are you sharing with your kids about your feelings regarding the LGBTQIA+ community?
2. If you suspect your kid may be LGBTQIA+, how are you letting them know that you are open and available for them to talk with you about their sexual orientation or gender identity?

3. If your kid came out to you today, what are the initial feelings that would come up for you?

4. What types of support do you have for yourself as you travel the journey of your kid's coming-out process?

5. What is the most powerful and supportive reaction you can have when your kid first comes out? *I will give you that answer as there is only one approach. The most supportive and powerful reaction you can have to your child coming out is to simply hug them tight and let them know that you love them.*

CHAPTER 4

A Deeper Dive into Supporting Transgender Kids

We've reached the point in our conversation where it's time to talk about supporting transgender and non-binary kids. Before we do, it is important for me to make something crystal clear. I am a cisgender queer man. I do not have lived experience as a trans or non-binary person. It is my solemn commitment to be as respectful, curious, and knowledgeable as I can about the lived experience of trans and non-binary people, but it is not my personal experience. My knowledge and the information I will share with you is based on years of research, training, consultation with transgender colleagues, personal interaction and relationships with transgender friends and acquaintances, and, most importantly, the honor of working with hundreds of transgender kids in the course of my work. I freely acknowledge that while my experience as a cis queer man in our society may share some parallels and similarities with the experiences of trans and non-binary people, our paths and experiences are not identical or interchangeable. I cannot and will not claim the unique singular experience of being transgender or non-binary in this world.

The best I or any of us can do is to listen, empathize, and remain curious and open to what trans and non-binary people have to tell us about themselves and their journeys. However, as I have devoted my professional life to supporting trans and non-binary kids, along with all the other sexual and gender identities out there, I believe it is vital to provide you as a parent with information that will assist you in understanding, supporting, and affirming your trans or non-binary kid on their coming-out journey. I have conceived this chapter as an "introduction to transgender care and support 101," recognizing that in-depth exploration and discussion of the nuances of the trans and non-binary experience could fill several books. This chapter is not intended to be a comprehensive guide to everything there is to know about being trans or non-binary. Rather, it is meant to serve as a starting point for parents of trans and non-binary kids as you begin a much longer path of education and discovery.

At the start of this book, we explored the concepts of biological sex, gender, gender identity, and gender expression. If you're still a little fuzzy on those, take a moment, return to Chapter 1 and give yourself a little refresher. I'll be here when you get back.

For the purposes of our discussion, and as a reminder, I want to make sure you are clear on the terms I am using here to describe gender identity and expression.

- The term transgender describes a person whose sex assigned at birth based on observable anatomy does not match the authentic gender identity they feel and know themselves to be inside.
- The term non-binary describes a person whose gender identity and expression do not conform to traditional constructs of male and female, masculine and feminine. Non-binary people generally do not feel affinity, or sometimes experience shifting affinities, with male and female/masculine and feminine traits, characteristics, roles, and forms of expression.

In the case of both transgender and non-binary people, their authentic gender identity and expression exist independently of their anatomy and sex assigned at birth. As we previously discussed, their sexual orientation also exists independently of their gender identity and expression.

Assigned sex versus gender identity

When children are first born, a well-meaning doctor will examine the baby and assign a sex solely based on the appearance of external sex organs. Yet children themselves are not born knowing what it means to be a girl or a boy. The gender stories they learn are based on social constructs that are erected by their parents, families, older children, and the people they observe around them. This training in gender is visible in every aspect of their daily existence, from the clothes they wear to the toys they are given to play with. Gender constructs grow stronger as they enter school, where nearly every aspect of their daily routine is influenced by their perceived gender. As puberty eventually arrives with changing bodies and emerging urges and feelings, the expectation of conformity to norms of masculine and feminine expression grows even more rigid and constraining.

The ever-increasing pressure placed on kids to adhere to gender constructs can feel suffocating even for some cisgender straight kids. Imagine what it's like for trans and non-binary kids who know deep down that the sex assigned to them at birth does not match who they truly are inside. This disparity is the beginning of what is most often a long and painful struggle to understand and embrace their authentic self, and then to find the strength and space to express that authentic self to the world, sometimes with profound consequences. As a parent, this can be a particularly difficult and painful process to witness, and an even more challenging one to support your kid through. You may observe your kid embracing more traditionally masculine traits, feminine traits, some of both, or a complete rejection of those limiting concepts. This may happen for some time before your kid is ever able, willing, or interested in putting a label on themselves or their journey; or your kid may try on several labels before they find what feels right for them. As a means of support and encouragement, and to give your kid space to explore and express themselves, I encourage you to think of gender as a spectrum of expression that is not necessarily connected to anatomy. Acknowledge that gender is a more expansive story than the one you may have grown up with. As I've encouraged you to do throughout this book, remain curious, neutral, and without judgment. Perhaps more than any other LGBTQIA+ people, trans and non-binary kids have so much to uncover and understand about themselves. It is a process of discovery and experimentation that will occur over years, could take numerous forms and unexpected turns, and may continue to evolve over the course of their entire lives. Your job is to let go of your attachments to who you thought your kid was and who you envisioned they would become so you can meet them as they are right now and keep meeting them as they work to inhabit their fully realized and authentic self.

There is one vital fact, supported by mountains of current research, that I hope will encourage and assist you to cultivate an affirming mindset toward your transgender or non-binary child. The fact is that gender- and identity-affirming behavior on the part of parents and other adults greatly improves the current and future mental health and well-being of transgender and non-binary kids. Just one person in their life who is affirming and understanding of their gender identity can make a huge difference and might even save their life. Trans youth are at particularly high risk for substance use, depression, anxiety, social rejection, and suicide. Between 40 and 50 percent of trans kids attempt suicide and these numbers skyrocket when we factor in race and socio-economic status.

One of the reasons that mental health and emotional well-being can be so challenging for transgender and non-binary kids is that they often walk through their days in a heightened state of anxiety and vigilance, sometimes to a greater degree than other LGBTQIA+ kids. Imagine that every waking moment of your day is spent working to hide your identity, monitoring your mannerisms, and censoring yourself. Almost all the kids I have worked with over the years report experiencing an uncomfortable and omnipresent negative voice in their heads that tells them they are not okay. That internal voice is what we call gender dysphoria, and it is driven by the disconnect between the body your transgender kid is walking around in and their internal sense of who they truly are. It is an ongoing daily struggle attempting to be gender normative and fulfilling the roles that are expected of them by friends, school environments, community standards, and even you, their well-meaning parents. When experienced continuously over years, it can have a profound negative impact on emotional, mental, and physical health.

Once a trans or non-binary kid comes out, that voice can become even more pronounced due to the added attention they are likely to receive. For trans and non-binary kids, the constant chatter of gender dysphoria can make it seem as though every moment of their day there is a loud, raucous soundtrack playing on repeat in their head. It interferes with their ability to concentrate, connect, and be present in their activities and interactions. The constant chatter is often characterized by anxious and stressful thoughts like "Am I fitting in?" "Are people staring at me?" "Are they going to call me by my real name?" "Am I about to be misgendered?" "Did I pick an outfit that looks right for my gender?" "Am I safe?" "Are those people going to bully me? Hurt me?" "Is there a bathroom I can use?" "Why does my voice sound like that?" "Is there a safe place I can escape to?" And on and on it goes. The intensity of gender dysphoria can be influenced by external factors but also by your kid's internal strength, which can vary from moment to moment. Even the strongest transgender kids, in the most affirming families, share that the internal negative voice may get quieter, but it never completely goes away.

Coming out and social transitioning

We have established that there are certain cultural norms that dictate "acceptable" gender expression based on the rules of the society one is born into. For transgender and non-binary kids, these norms feel uncomfortable, confining, restrictive, and wrong. As I mentioned, this feeling of wrongness is known as gender dysphoria. Sometimes it takes time for a trans or non-binary kid to reach the point where they understand that the feelings they are experiencing are due to gender dysphoria and that stepping outside society's expectations and letting their true identity dictate their outward gender expression is how they can begin to reconcile their inner and outer selves. Some people are well into adulthood before they realize this, while others understand it in early childhood.

Many of the kids I work with take their first steps toward living authentically by initiating a process called social transition. This is a period in which the primary aspects of their authentic gender identity are explored and expressed through means that do not include any type of medical intervention. The facets of social transition expressed by many trans kids include coming out as their authentic gender, initiating a change of name and pronouns, changing how they dress and groom themselves, altering which socially gendered activities they participate in, and taking body-shifting actions such as binding, packing, or tucking.

The point at which a trans or non-binary kid initiates social transitioning can be challenging for parents. It is the point where you actually have to face the music and witness your kid let go of the persona you've been used to for their whole life up to this point. They will start to look, sound, act, and even smell differently from the kid you've always known. They may choose to change the name you chose for them when they were born, something that can be particularly difficult for some parents. To support and affirm your trans or non-binary kid's coming-out process, you must prepare yourself to become acquainted with a new authentically realized version of your kid that includes their real gender identity, which they have probably been fighting, hiding, and restraining for years. While it will naturally take time and effort for you to adjust to these changes, including giving yourself the space and time to grieve for the dreams and vision you had of who and what your kid would grow up to be, resolve to love and embrace the enhanced and expanded manifestation of your kid as their true identity emerges. Find anticipation and excitement in the privilege you are being granted to meet your kid as they truly are. Support your kid as they make the changes that feel right for them. Find the strength and patience to be flexible if your kid decides to make adjustments or change course. You may have trouble meeting them with perfect equanimity and neutrality on every step of this path of social transition and that is okay. As we've discussed over and over, there will be missteps, mistakes, disagreements, and obstacles, but what is most important is that you don't give up. Ultimately, it is their path to follow and with or without your support, they are going to pursue these changes. One of the most powerful ways you can demonstrate your support is through committed ongoing recognition of their name and pronouns. Be willing to take them shopping so they can find the clothing that expresses to the world who they are. If they want to alter their hairstyle, assist them in finding a stylist who can make that happen. I sometimes accompany my clients on rehearsal shopping trips and it is amazing to watch them light up as they shop in the stores and aisles where they can find clothing that expresses to the world their authentic self.

Self-affirmation: binders, packers, tucking, and bras

When I introduced the concept of social transitioning in the last section, I mentioned binding, packing, and tucking. These are words you might not be familiar with. These are practices that some trans and non-binary people use to physically affirm and express their gender identity. The first of these practices is binding. A binder is a constrictive piece of clothing that a trans male or non-binary person will wear underneath their shirt to lessen the appearance of breasts and compress their chest. Binders can be uncomfortable and take some getting used to, so it is important that you support your child and assist them in purchasing a well-fitting binder. There are many transgender affirmative online companies that can help with this process, guiding you and your kid through taking proper measurements, choosing the best type of binder, proper care, and how to wear it so it feels right. Know that your kid will most likely be wearing their binder every day so if it is financially feasible, purchase more than one so your kid can keep them clean. Some quick safety notes about binders:

- They are not meant to be worn for more than eight hours a day.
- It is not advisable to engage in strenuous exercise while wearing a binder.
- Binders are not meant to be slept in.

It is not uncommon for trans or non-binary kids who feel compelled to bind their chests to initially explore using ace bandages or even duct tape to bind. These are not healthy long-term options and can cause pain and damage to a kid's body. A binder may seem like a foreign or even extreme piece of clothing to you but for your transgender child it can provide a deep sense of comfort, well-being, and self-affirmation.

Some transgender male kids may express interest in packing as a means of expressing their authentic self. Packing is the act of simulating the presence of a penis and testicles by inserting something into underwear to produce a bulge. Many kids will simply use a sock stuffed artfully into their underwear to enhance their bulge. A powerful way to assist them in this moment is to purchase briefs, boxers, or whatever style of underwear will help them feel comfortable. Some trans kids may want to purchase a packer, a silicone penis designed specifically for this purpose, to further the illusion, especially when puberty sets in. There are numerous online resources that offer products designed to meet this need. Your kid may or may not want to pursue this as part of their social transition but keep the door open as their needs evolve.

It is common for trans female kids who are beginning social transitioning to start wearing clothes designed for girls and women. Where trans male kids may want to enhance their bulge, trans female kids may want to diminish theirs. Tucking is one method of achieving this. As the name implies, tucking is simply the act of tucking the penis and testicles down between the legs to reduce the extent to which they protrude from the body. There are styles of underwear known as gaffs that are specifically designed to aid in this process. Some trans female kids may seek out online information about ways of making their bodies look more feminine and find information online about tucking using things like duct tape, a method rumored to be used by some drag queens. This is not a safe or healthy method of tucking and should be avoided.

Just as trans male kids may want to diminish the appearance of breasts, trans female kids may want to enhance the appearance of breasts on their bodies. This can easily be achieved by purchasing an appropriately sized bra and using socks or some other method of filling to simulate breasts. One method used widely in the modeling and entertainment industries, as well as by many cisgender women, is what are known colloquially as "chicken cutlets." These are silicone inserts designed to be placed inside a bra to enhance the size and shape of breasts. They are widely available online in various shapes and sizes.

There is no set order for how your kid may explore their social transition, and they will often initiate the process with changes that have a smaller impact and then as they get braver and more comfortable, graduate to larger impact expressions. With your affirmation and support this can be a beautiful process to witness as your trans or non-binary kid blossoms into their authentic self. Because all these techniques of social transition are completely reversible, many parents find them to be challenging but manageable steps in their own journey of embracing their trans or non-binary kid's transition. These steps are often helpful in preparing parents for the next potentially more substantial stages of their kid's transition.

Medical transition

The phase of transition where many parents find themselves triggered, concerned, and overwhelmed is when their child desires to initiate the process of medical transition. For most kids, this will be the point at which they desire to initiate hormone-affirming therapy to align their body more completely with their gender. It is important to take some time here and explore why this moment is so triggering for many parents. As a parent, your number one job since your child was born has been to keep them safe and healthy. Then they approach you about using a medical procedure to alter the body that you have been focused on protecting for their whole life. Your fear and resistance are a natural response and, in my experience, are often a part of the grief process we discussed earlier. Take some time and find the support you need to unpack these feelings, fears, and concerns away from your child so that you can then begin to educate yourself on the value of supporting your transgender child in their pursuit of gender-affirming therapies.

Yes, I am encouraging you to let your trans kid take the lead and to follow the path they are setting out for you. Work with an experienced trans-affirming therapist and/or support group to help you with your own needs and connect with a physician who is well versed in the care of transgender youth to safely make a plan for your trans kid's transition. Myriad studies, research, and personal anecdotes point to the conclusion that for the mental, emotional, and physical well-being of your trans kid it is important that you support them in their pursuit of gender-affirming therapies. In my practice, I have found that much of the depression, anxiety, gender dysphoria, and suicidality that trans and non-binary kids go through is in direct correlation to the discomfort they experience in the bodies they have found themselves in since birth. This can be addressed through medical support that helps them alter their bodies in ways that affirm their authentic self. Hormone therapy can radically improve quality of life and emotional and mental health for trans kids. While this is a big ask that may require you to step way outside your comfort zone, as a parent who ultimately wants the best for your kid, you should approach this phase of your kid's transition with openness.

Knowledge is power, so I am going to provide a basic introduction to the three most common approaches to gender-affirming hormone therapy in the hope that it will encourage you to explore all the options more fully and gain the knowledge you and your kid need to decide on the right path for them. And I can't stress enough the importance of finding a qualified physician who specializes in gender-affirming therapies to guide you both along the way.

Depending on how old your transgender/non-binary child is, one of these first approaches to affirming care is the use of puberty blockers, which do pretty much what the name implies; they block the hormones released by the pituitary gland that trigger puberty. Kids who are placed on puberty blockers simply won't go through puberty and all the body changes that take place during that process will be temporarily delayed. Puberty blockers are most effective for kids if started either before or early in the process of puberty, where they will simply pause the process. If puberty has already begun, blockers can assist older trans kids in managing some of the more dysphoric body processes such as having erections or menstruation.

Puberty blockers are typically administered as injections, either monthly or every three months, and while taking puberty blockers, your child will have regular blood tests to monitor the medication's effectiveness. Your doctor will usually monitor for any side effects, which are few and rare. Most trans and non-binary children take the medication for a few years, though your doctor will prescribe the approach that is best for your kid knowing that each child is different. One of the best things about puberty blockers is they give you and your child time to explore their goals in medical transition and to work with a medical provider to develop a proactive plan focusing on those goals. Once puberty blockers are stopped, the body will renew its developmental progress into puberty.

Another reason that I personally support responsible doctor-supervised use of puberty blockers is that puberty is a challenging process for anybody and for a trans/non-binary kid even more so. By using puberty blockers, we hit the pause button on the process of puberty, so a transgender kid is not forced to go through puberty twice in their lifetime, once as the biological sex they were assigned at birth and again during the process of initiating hormone-affirming therapy. In working with parents who are confused and concerned about this process, I often ask them if they would want to go through puberty more than once and that seems to get the point across. So, would you want to go through puberty more than once?

After suppressing puberty for a few years, the next step will happen when your child decides to stop puberty-blocking therapy or pursue other hormone-affirming treatments. This is a moment when you will probably hit another parental concern roadblock. At this point, I encourage you to realize that starting hormone therapy is not a decision that your kid is taking lightly. This move toward medical transition is something they crave and need at a core level to affirm themselves in their true identity. Most of the kids I work with have researched this process and know what it entails. I encourage you to have candid and frequent discussions with your trans or non-binary kid about what the process means to them, what they hope to achieve, and what they want you to know about their reasons for pursuing it. Share the knowledge you have gained to ensure that you are both on the same page.

For a trans feminine or non-binary kid who is pursuing a more feminine appearance, the next step in their process is to take estrogen and an androgen blocker. You may be familiar with estrogen but not so sure about androgen blockers. These are simply drugs that block the testosterone that a body assigned male at birth may be producing. To start the process, your kid's doctor will want to run blood work to get a baseline reading on current hormone levels, cholesterol levels, and liver and kidney functions that will assist them in determining the best approach for achieving your kid's desired results while also protecting their health.

Estrogen is available in several forms, including pills, gels, patches, and injections, while androgen blockers are administered in pill form. A lot of kids prefer a pill format for both, so it is easier to take everything together. Estrogen has a number of effects on the body, including breast development, fat redistribution, and the softening of skin. At the same time, the androgen blocker will decrease muscle mass, shrink testicles, diminish the occurrence of erections, and reduce facial hair. Some of these changes will become noticeable around six months after the start of hormone-affirming therapy but will often not be fully realized for up to 24 months.

Trans masculine or non-binary kids who are pursuing a more masculine presentation will start the process by taking testosterone, or as it is more commonly referred to, T. The effects of taking testosterone include the growth of body hair, redistribution of fat and muscle, alterations in facial structure, lowering of the voice, changes in skin including texture, thickness, and oiliness, and the lessening or complete cessation of menstruation. Most of these changes will become visible within the first four to six months and will continue to progress for the next 12–18 months Typically, your kid's doctor will prescribe a low dose to start and slowly increase the dosage over a period of months to find the right balance for your kid's body. Testosterone is given either by self-injection or a gel applied to the skin, with the former being more efficacious. Similar to starting estrogen, your kid's doctor will want to run blood work to get a baseline reading on current hormone levels, cholesterol levels, and liver and kidney functions that will assist them in providing the best care for your child.

You may have heard rumors of or found references online to the mythological rage and extreme mood swings alleged to accompany starting testosterone, or "T." In my years of experience, what I witness the most from kids starting testosterone is happiness, lowered anxiety, calmness, and a deep sense of rightness. Changes in mood/behaviors based on hormone therapy are often similar to what your child would be going through with puberty if their body naturally produced the amount/kind of these specific hormones that matched their gender identity. It's an adjustment to all involved. If in the rare instance that you notice dramatic mood swings and personality changes, talk to your kid and their doctor, and explore adjusting their dose or the manner in which they are taking T.

Gender-affirming surgery

In my experience of working with parents of trans and non-binary kids, discussions of gender-affirming surgery are the most likely to produce anxiety, panic, and resistance due to the finality of these solutions. If you are finding this to be true for you, stay with me, keep breathing, take a moment if you need to, and we can make it through this together.

The next and often most considered phase of medical transition, both by parents and transgender and non-binary people, is surgery. Standards vary from country to country, but most surgical procedures occur after a person has turned 18. Once again, I know from my work with parents that this is probably the moment where all your biggest fears and concerns about the well-being of your child are coming to the forefront. It is important to know that for most transgender people, surgery is often the last step in their process of transition. It is also the step to which they have devoted the most thought, contemplation, research, and soul-searching. Some trans/non-binary people achieve their most affirmed self without the need for surgery, while for others this is an essential and necessary step in their journey toward affirmation of their gender identity. Understand that surgical procedures can assist many transgender people in feeling at ease and present in their bodies, as well as presenting to the world the best version of themselves.

Some of these most common surgeries for gender affirmation include:

- Facial reconstruction surgery, which can make a face look more feminine, masculine, or androgynous, as aligns best with a person's gender identity and expression. These procedures may include fillers, injections, and surgical procedures that enhance and alter the face to achieve desired results.
- Hair removal procedures. There are many permanent methods of hair removal that trans and non-binary people can pursue to achieve an appearance that best reflects their gender identity and expression.
- Chest surgery or "top" surgery, where a surgeon may either remove or enhance breast tissue to achieve the size and shape of the chest that best aligns with a person's gender identity and expression.
- Gender-affirmation surgery or "bottom surgery," which is the term used to describe procedures that transform and rebuild genitals so they align as closely as possible in appearance and function with a person's gender identity and expression.

I hope you are still breathing and understand that these types of procedures may be the best option for the spiritual, emotional, physical, and mental well-being of your trans kid. As I mentioned, pursuing these solutions is usually the result of extensive research, discussion, and consultation with experienced trans-affirming medical professionals, and years of personal development and soul-searching. They are not something you sign up for the moment your kid comes out as trans or non-binary. I work from a model of care that is called informed consent, and its most basic tenet is that each person has the right to define and affirm their gender in the ways that feel most authentic and appropriate for them. If you can move through your fears and anxieties, educate yourself, and find the right support, then you will have created the foundation you need to stand up as an advocate for your trans or non-binary kid's well-being, and act as a valued asset to their care team.

For most transgender and non-binary people, the support of their families, partners, friends, and loved ones can ease their journey through affirming their gender identity. Gestures like visiting the doctor by their side to ask important questions they may forget to ask in their anxiousness, shopping with them as they pick out the perfect outfit they have been longing to wear for years, and being there to hold their hand as they wake up in the hospital after surgery will deepen the bond between you and open your heart as you help bring your kid into the world for the second time.

Questions for contemplation

1. How have you noticed the social constructs of gender affecting your child?
2. How would it feel for you to walk around every moment of every day with a raucous soundtrack of negative self-talk clamoring in your head?
3. What aspects of social transition feel uncomfortable for you and why?
4. What are the biggest fears that arise in you at the prospect of medical transition?
5. What steps are you ready to take to educate yourself in how to best support your trans or non-binary kid?

CHAPTER 5

The Cornerstones of Support

S o, now it's happened. Your brave, wonderful, beautiful child has for the first time spoken the words out loud, revealing their sexual orientation or gender identity to you. Maybe this is no surprise and you've been imagining and preparing for this moment since they were three years old. Maybe somewhere in the back of your mind you suspected and wondered but didn't let yourself think about it too much. Maybe it came completely out of the blue and you're reeling, feeling blindsided, shocked, and off balance. No matter the circumstances, this moment of honesty is the beginning of a journey that will run the gamut from joyous highs to sorrowful lows. But with a little awareness, openness, some practical tools, and support, you and your kid can both grow through this experience, creating an even closer family connection.

As you've learned, the coming-out process for LGBTQIA+ kids can be terrifying, not only for them but also for you. As your kid reveals their true self to you, you are going to experience a hurricane of emotions that can range from concern, confusion, shock, disbelief, rejection, and anger to peace, understanding, acceptance, relief, and pride. The number one piece of advice I offer to parents as they ride out these emotional experiences is to commit to kindness. We've established that this is a particularly vulnerable time for you, your kid, and your whole family. Making kindness your default response to the situations you are bound to face as your kid comes out, even when—in fact *especially* when—you aren't being met with kindness in return, will help you lay the foundation for a future relationship based on mutual respect, openness, support, and love.

Committing to kindness and making it a habit while your kid is learning how to define and integrate with their sexual orientation and/or gender identity is your best defense against deterioration of communication and erosion of trust in your relationship. Believe me, I know this isn't always an easy thing to do. In the heat of the moment, when you and your kid may both be feeling insecure, angry, and confused and you're confronted with harsh words or attitude, taking a breath, centering yourself, and responding with kindness requires strength and control. It takes practice, focus, and presence of mind. You may not succeed every time. You will make mistakes. But what is important is that you don't give up. Take responsibility for your mistakes and missteps. Admit when you're wrong and apologize, even if you're not the *only* one who was wrong. Ultimately, you're the adult. However your kid is engaging with you, they are looking for your guidance, even if they won't admit it or show it. Even when they're lashing out, your kid is watching and learning from your responses, reactions, and decisions. Teaching by example during these tumultuous and trying moments can be a supreme test of patience and character but persevering and committing to kindness can make a huge impact on the strength of your current and future relationship, while also teaching your LGBTQIA+ kid that they can trust you to be there for them no matter what.

I've often encountered situations in my work when in the

lead-up to or just after an LGBTQIA+ kid has come out, their parents will come to me in distress because the sweet, happy, gentle kid they used to know has suddenly been replaced by a moody, confrontational monster they don't recognize. This is the point where the conversation about committing to kindness usually starts. But as we discussed earlier, it's also important to remember that the process of coming out usually begins well before you hear it from your kid. It often begins with the sharing of feelings with a close friend or trusted family member who isn't a parent, someone who presents a lower risk where they can give their coming out a test run. Although coming out is a normal step in the development of an LGBTQIA+ adolescent, many potentially frightening thoughts and questions can come to the forefront for your child:

- Why am I questioning my sexual identity or gender identity, or both?
- Who can I trust in this process?
- Will my family and friends accept this new information?
- Will I be safe sharing this information with others?

With all these questions and others swirling around an LGBTQIA+ kid's mind, it may be challenging to come out in a well-thought-out and structured manner. The coming-out conversation may be a reaction to other issues or may be presented in a confrontational manner.

At first, your teen may not even be sure of their sexuality and gender and may struggle to define and communicate their experience in a clear and concise way. Understand that their minds are busy exploring their own confusion, comparing themselves with other teens and what they're seeing online and in the media as a means of figuring out who they are. For some kids, this process of discovery moves quickly as they begin to be comfortable in their affirmed identity, while others may travel through a darker journey, which can lead to isolation and a negative self-concept.

As parents, it is important to create a supportive environment for your LGBTQIA+ child to communicate about what's going on inside them. Although it may be challenging for you to have these conversations, it is just as hard for them to share this new authentic identity with you because they are often still questioning their own feelings.

So, what can you do to make this conversation a little easier for all of you? First, as I mentioned at the top of this chapter, lead with kindness, both for your kid and yourself. For even the most well-informed families, the initial moments of coming out can lead to a lot of confusion and challenging interactions. There are going to be misunderstandings that will lead to hurt feelings often followed by the phrase, "you just don't get it!" And they may be right, you don't get it! And that's okay. Rather than trying to defend yourself and your preconceptions, acknowledge your ignorance, your inexperience, your inability to walk in their shoes. Commit to responding with kindness, care, and love. Nurture a space where it's okay for both you and your kid to be confused and ask them to do the same. It's fine to not know. The key is finding whatever means you can to communicate that you are fully invested in loving your LGBTQIA+ kid while you *both* figure things out.

As fraught as these moments can get, one of the best ways to keep that energy of kindness available is to focus on techniques that will assist you in staying calm and centered. Coming out can be a shock for all of you that doesn't necessarily end after the initial moment when the words are spoken. Leave space for further thought in conversations so that you don't always feel on the spot to react immediately. If things get too heated or confusing, take a little break. Step away and practice a moment of self-care, while encouraging your kid to do the same. Take a breath, decompress with your partner, take a walk, play with the dog, listen to music, whatever tools work for you to soften your reactivity and reconnect you to that kindness I keep emphasizing.

One suggestion I'll share about breaks is this: don't just walk away. Instead, make it an intentional process. Let your kid know that you are getting a little overwhelmed and need a few moments to collect yourself. Do your best not to make this a dramatic gesture that leaves your kid feeling that you can't stand them anymore and have to get away from them. Rather, make sure they know that you want your talk to be civil, respectful, and productive, so you're going to take a few minutes to make sure that happens from your end. Give them a time frame and stick to it. "I need us to take a break for a moment. Let's continue this conversation in 30 minutes." Decompress for 30 minutes in whatever manner works best for you, and then check in with your kid again and see how they are. This cooling-off period will assist both of you in gathering your thoughts, dialing back your stress, and approaching each other in a loving and respectful manner. It may not always work. Your kid may derail your efforts. You may lose your temper. But as I said before, the key is that you don't give up.

The love and respect that committing to kindness can culti-vate goes a long way toward smoothing the rough edges for you and your kid during intense conversations. Even when things get overwhelming or challenging, remaining supportive and letting them know how much you love them for exactly who they are can make the difference between extended conflict and a momentary flare-up. Remember also, that for most adolescents, the angst of being a teen and figuring out their identity is a vital period in their lives when they literally lay the foundation for the adults they are becoming. That's why it is so important to be patient with them as they explore what being LGBTQIA+ means to them. It may shift and evolve as they become more aware of the emerging facets of their LGBTQIA+ identity and have opportunities to test out what they like, what they don't like, what feels natural, and what feels forced. Instead of attempting to put them in an identity box that is comfortable for you, commit to being curious about who they are as their LGBTQIA+ identity emerges and integrates into their overall identity.

Committing to curiosity is a tool you can use in your efforts to be the supportive parent you want to be for your LGBTQIA+ child. Even as you are reading these pages, LGBTQIA+ definitions and identities are shifting, expanding, and evolving. Just as it's important to give yourself permission to not know everything about LGBTQIA+ identity development, give your kid space and permission to not have all the answers about what their gender identity or sexual orientation means to them. They are undoubtedly exploring how the various labels, characteristics, and flavors of expression resonate with them, and the process of experimentation may continue beyond their adolescence and into adulthood. Reminding yourself to be curious about their evolution, rather than rigid about their identity, will be a powerful asset in your efforts to be present and affirming with your child. Learning from them as they learn from themselves can be a profound bonding experience for both of you.

An important concept for you to understand and then communicate to your kid during your discussions about their LGBTQIA+ identity is that you realize this journey will lead to important discoveries. Some of them will be exciting and joyous, while others will be uncomfortable and confusing. These discoveries will influence your kid's willingness to communicate and may even impact their ability to do so as they come to terms with the barrage of new information they are processing. Some days your kid may be approachable and happy to communicate, other days they may need to have space to be contemplative, to move deep inside themselves and sit with their thoughts. While this inconsistency may feel like a rollercoaster of frustration and unpredictability to you, recognize and do your best to ride out these challenging moments with them. Don't feel as if you have to push. When your kid has a day, week, or maybe even a month where they have no interest in sharing and processing, let that be okay. Through your actions, intentions, and words, demonstrate to them that they are in a safe environment where they are loved and affirmed. That atmosphere of support will help keep the channels of communication open when they are ready to open up.

Most of the parents I work with express that one of their biggest concerns for their LGBTQIA+ child is the bullying and harassment they may be experiencing, especially at school. Check in regularly with your child to uncover any threats they may be facing to their personal safety at school. Encourage them to speak with you or another safe adult about any teasing, bullying, or harassment they encounter. Knowing where a safe space exists at their school is a key factor for LGBTQIA+ kids to maintain their sense of personal safety. As a parent, you will be walking a fine line when working with your kid's school between wanting to be proactive in guaranteeing the safety of your LGBTQIA+ child and respecting their need for autonomy, space, and privacy. I suggest meeting with decision makers at your kid's school to learn where they stand on developing and enforcing LGBTQIA+-affirming policies and guidelines. This could be a difficult thing to do if your child has not given their permission for you to intercede since by bringing up these topics you run the risk of outing them to adults at their school. Communicating with your school's administration on no-bullying policies while learning more about the LGBTQIA+ student support systems is important, both in terms of keeping their school accountable and in understanding the atmosphere your kid is experiencing at school. But it is also a step that should be taken with care, sensitivity, and an appreciation for the risks that could accompany such conversations if you encounter unsympathetic or hostile viewpoints.

There is an important aspect of the coming-out process that in my experience as a therapist is one of the most overlooked and surprising for parents of LGBTQIA+ kids. It's natural that parents focus their energy and attention on their LGBTQIA+ kid as they navigate coming out and the inevitable consequences and adjustments that follow. What parents often overlook is the need to turn their focus from their kid's journey to their own from time to time. Your kid is not the only one whose life is transforming, and you will find that you need to pause and reassess your own belief systems, especially as they relate to gender identity and sexual orientation. It is fascinating to reflect that LGBTQIA+ children are one of a handful of minorities that are raised in a household where their minority status is usually not represented in the family structure. Most LGBTQIA+ kids are being raised in cisgender, heteronormative households and do not see their LGBTQIA+ identity modeled in their parents. If you are a cisgender heterosexual parent, it is rare that you have had to examine your own personal feelings and beliefs about gender and sexual orientation any deeper than considering how you react to what you see or read in the news. This means that you have a greater responsibility and perhaps a somewhat tougher path to gain the knowledge required to understand and empathize with your kid's LGBTQIA+ experience. Reflecting, understanding, and facing your own ignorance, biases, assumptions, and misconceptions can be challenging but if you are willing to open your mind and your heart, let go of your attachment to the comforting paradigms you grew up with, and be open to learning, the experience can be transformative, giving you the best chance of success in supporting your kid now and throughout their life.

As you become more and more informed and aware, you will

also unravel some of the most common intrusive thoughts that parents experience as they witness their child's emerging identity. Many parents carry misconceptions about gender identity and sexual orientation and find themselves in a self-destructive spiral of uninformed thoughts. A common thought that many parents land on is "it's just a phase." I'm here to tell you it is not. When a kid is brave enough to unveil their LGBTQIA+ identity to you, it is something they have been feeling and contemplating for a long time. How they express it may vary and evolve as we have discussed, but their underlying identity is a constant that needs to be respected and affirmed. The "it's a phase" mentality does not respect your LGBTQIA+ child's autonomy in discovering who they are and how they want to walk through their world.

Other parents get stuck in the search for a "cure." I am once again here to tell you that not only is there no cure, there is nothing to cure. Your kid's LGBTQIA+ identity is not something that can nor needs to be fixed. The complete opposite is true. Their LGBTQIA+ identity is something that should be nurtured, expanded, supported, and affirmed. I beg you as a parent who loves your child to release any notion of needing to fix your LGBTQIA+ kid. Instead, with each thought, word, and action, deepen your love and support and affirm who they are.

I also beg you not to search for a reason, action, or experience to blame as the cause of your kid's LGBTQIA+ identity. This type of "what did I do wrong" or "if only I had" thinking is harmful to your kid's identity development and is the opposite of creating a safe space for them and the rest of the family during the coming-out process. The fact is, we don't know why people are lesbian, gay, straight, transgender, or bisexual. Most likely, LGBTQIA+ identities are the result of a complex and unpredictable interplay of genetic, physiological, hormonal, and environmental influences, and not the result of a choice. Rather than dwelling on why your kid is who they are, focus your energy where you can be most productive and make a positive difference in your kid's life, which is to create a safe, loving, affirming environment where they can grow and develop into the authentic incandescent human being they were always meant to be.

My guess is that if you are reading this book, it means that you are actively seeking knowledge and resources to help you and your kid through the challenging and unknown territory where you find yourselves. You should be commended for taking steps to learn and understand. That takes courage and says a lot about you as a parent. In addition to the knowledge you'll gain from this book, which will give you a great foundation for supporting your LGBTQIA+ kid, I can't say enough about the benefit of exploring and taking advantage of the resources that are available in your community to add another layer of support for your entire family. Connecting to community and engaging with others who have or are going through similar experiences, challenges, and discoveries to you can be a huge help in alleviating the anxiety and stress that are often present as part of the coming-out process. Often, when we are moving though any type of challenging time in our lives, we feel as if we are going through it alone and it's hard to believe that anyone else understands it. This feeling of isolation is something you may be feeling and by reaching out for community resources aimed at supporting and informing parents, you will find that there are other families out there, just like yours, that are going through the same or similar experiences. This connection will assist in dismissing the isolation that you may be feeling and help you to feel supported by a community which will have experience and knowledge, and sometimes can just be a sounding board for all the thoughts and feelings racing around inside you.

And if this community, grassroots approach to support doesn't feel as if it is giving you all the processing space that you need, I

suggest finding your own therapist who is qualified in supporting families during the coming-out process. It can be a challenge
to be open and available for your LGBTQIA+ child when you are
simultaneously trying to address your own fears, concerns, and
emotions. Consider therapy with a qualified counselor who works
with LGBTQIA+ kids and their families during the coming-out
process. Therapy can provide a forum for parents to ask questions,
gather information and ease their emotional distress in a neutral
environment. It is also an opportunity to share and process some
of the dark thoughts and fears you may be experiencing so that
you can avoid falling into the trap of blame and questioning why.
When looking for the right therapist, you will discover that there
are many "gay friendly" therapists, but that's not the same thing as
someone who is trained in the specific issues and nuances faced by
LGBTQIA+ people and their families during the coming-out process. I believe it is important to find a therapist who specializes in
LGBTQIA+ affirmative therapy, who will have in-depth training and
experience to be present with and guide you through the coming-
out process. When searching for an affirming therapist, be willing
to ask them about their background, training, and experience in
working with the LGBTQIA+ community. It's okay to interview a
prospective therapist and make sure that they are the best fit for
you and your needs.

I hope that by now you are noticing a few consistent themes
about the practical steps you can take to support your LGBTQIA+
child. Be curious. Be thoughtful. Be present. Be patient. Put the
same focus and energy into taking care of yourself that you put
into taking care of your child. Most important of all, make kindness
and love the foundation of every conversation. Kindness and love
are the tools that will allow you and your kid to move through this
process together and face the challenging moments of the journey
with grace, honesty, and authenticity.

Questions for contemplation

1. What are your biggest fears when it comes to being able to support your LGBTQIA+ child?
2. How comfortable are you with not knowing when it comes to your kid's coming-out journey?
3. What, who, and where are potential sources of support for you during this coming-out process?
4. Are you blaming yourself for your kid's LGBTQIA+ identity or searching for a reason that this is who they are?
5. How can you release yourself from this way of thinking?

CHAPTER 6

You're Going Through a Process Too

When your kid comes out as LGBTQIA+, it's natural to direct all your focus onto your child and their needs. While your kid does need your focus and attention at this vulnerable time, focusing solely on them to the exclusion of all else, including your own needs and feelings, might actually mean setting yourself and your child up for a rougher, more tumultuous road ahead. In earlier chapters, we've discussed the need for giving yourself breaks and space when necessary. We've talked about giving yourself permission to make mistakes, to forgive yourself and not give up when they happen. What we have yet to discuss is allowing yourself the time and the space to grieve.

Now, you may be thinking: "Wait, allow myself to grieve? I thought I was supposed to be making this a safe, positive experience, affirming my kid's identity, and supporting them through their journey. How do grief and grieving fit into that?" I understand why you might think that. On the surface, it seems counterintuitive to encourage you to grieve when we've spent pages and pages talking about making your reaction to your kid's coming out positive and affirming. But the fact is, to fully embrace your child's LGBTQIA+

identity and be fully present and authentic with them in their coming-out process, you have to let go of your pre-existing notions of
who you thought they were, who you expected they would become,
and the life you expected they would live. Until you've done that, it's
unlikely that you'll be able to give your kid the honest and authentic
support and affirmation they need.

Just as you might be, the parents of LGBTQIA+ kids I work with
in my therapy practice are often surprised and sometimes puzzled
when I ask them if they have given themselves room to grieve as part
of their kid's coming-out process. After years of assisting families
as they take this journey together, I am firmly convinced of the key
role grieving plays in a parent's ability to support their LGBTQIA+
kid successfully and authentically. Psychologists have identified a
well-documented process that most people experience when faced
with a profound loss, commonly referred to as the stages of grief.
Most people associate grief with death but in psychology we have
come to understand that grief is a natural reaction to any event that
unexpectedly changes the expected course of one's life, especially if
it is an event that we feel we have no control or agency over. While
grief is a complex emotional journey that encompasses an array
of unique individual experiences, the process of grieving usually
follows a general pattern of five emotional stages: denial, anger, bargaining, depression, and acceptance. Time and again I have watched
parents experience variations of these emotional stages and I have
worked to help them acknowledge and understand them as they're
happening. Taking the opportunity to acknowledge your own grief,
be present with it, and process it as it runs its inevitable course can
mean the difference between a positive and negative coming-out
experience for both you and your kid.

What might you be grieving as the parent of an LGBTQIA+
kid? Well, if grief is a natural reaction to an event that changes
the expected course of your life, an event over which you have

no control or agency, then the realization that your kid's sexual and/or gender identity is something other than what you've spent their whole life believing it was, that their life is going to look markedly different from what you envisioned for them, must certainly qualify as a valid trigger for grief. But it's important to understand and identify the loss that you as a parent are grieving. Most often, the basis for the grief I witness in my office with parents of LGBTQIA+ kids, is the loss of the "dream" of their child. Think back to the moment when your child first came into your life, the moment when you first met that amazing, beautiful, radiant being who suddenly became a vital and irreplaceable part of your life. From that first moment, you probably started imagining and fantasizing about who and what that new little being would become. You probably imagined experiences you would observe or have with them, momentous achievements and firsts like their first steps, their first words, their first day of school, sports they might play, activities they might participate in, awards they might win, boyfriends or girlfriends they might have, graduations, weddings, careers, homes, family holidays, and the grandchildren they might give you. Naturally, your visions, hopes, and dreams for your new child were probably idealized and followed the accepted cisgender/heteronormative social and cultural models you were raised with. Your daughter would walk down the aisle, wearing a beautiful white dress and a veil, toward a handsome man in a tuxedo. She would have a successful career, happy, healthy children, a lovely home. Your son would be a great student and captain of a sports team. He'd meet a lovely girl, get married, and have happy, healthy children you would spoil and adore.

Then, that child whose future you've been envisioning and pouring all your hopes into since they came into your life comes out as LGBTQIA+ and the dream shatters. Suddenly the visions and fantasies you've indulged in and become attached to all these years are gone. It won't be a handsome man in a tuxedo your daughter is walking toward. Your son won't find a nice girl and settle down. Your daughter isn't actually your daughter, but your son, or vice versa, or neither. Most parents don't realize how dependent and attached they are to those fantasies and expectations until the moment when they crumble. The weight of parental expectations can be heavy for any child, whether they are LGBTQIA+ or not. But the loss of those parental dreams is often particularly poignant for parents of LGBTQIA+ kids. The reaction to that loss can be unexpectedly strong, which is why it is so important for you as the parent of an LGBTQIA+ kid to acknowledge your loss and be aware of your grief and its stages so you can process it in a healthy, supported way that doesn't transfer the blame and emotional weight of your loss to your kid.

So, what might that grief dialogue sound like in your head? Here are a few examples shared with me by various parents over the years:

Denial: "This is just a phase they are going through." "My teen played piano for years and then just gave it up. This is the same kind of thing." "They can't be transgender; they were on the football team for years." "They are too attractive to be asexual."

Anger: "I am not going to let them walk out of the house dressed like that." "It's my spouse's fault." "I am not going to pay for college if they go through with this transition." "God will punish you for your sins."

Bargaining: "If only I had been there more when they were growing up." "I will pray to God to take this burden away." "If I put them in a new school, this will all go away."

Depression: "I don't understand why this has happened to our family." "I just want to hide away and keep this all secret." "This is all too much."

Acceptance: "What can I do to help?" "What do you need from us to make your transition easier?" "I saw this Pride shirt and bought one for each of us." "I would love it if you had your friends over this weekend."

These are just a few of the more common comments that I hear from parents in my office, and each person will have their own journey through these moments of grief. Remember that grief is a unique and individual process and there is no correct way to experience the process. Although many people see grief as a linear process, I am here to tell you that it is not. It will have highs and lows, moments when you feel enlightened, moments when you feel overwhelmed, and moments when you are confused and unsure of your emotional state.

The important and somewhat subtle distinction I want to emphasize as you identify, acknowledge, and process your grief is that you are not grieving the loss of your child. Your child is still here, and they are the same person they have always been. Instead, you are grieving the loss of the dream you created and clung to of who your child would be. You are grieving the loss of something that never actually existed, something you wanted, hoped for, envisioned, but which was never actually real. And while the dream was never real, the feelings you are experiencing certainly are real. It is natural and valid for you as a parent to have these feelings and experiences when your kid comes out. They don't make you a bad person or a bad parent. What is important is that you work on a healthy way to process and experience your feelings of grief without directing them at your kid. Before your kid came out, they likely envisioned every possible scenario of how the revelation of their sexual and/or gender identity might play out, from a scene of loving acceptance to one of violent rejection. They probably spent months, or maybe even years agonizing over what would happen and how you'd react when the truth finally came out. Your kid is almost certainly aware of the hopes and dreams you have for them. For LGBTQIA+ kids, a great deal of the stress of coming out is often connected to the pain of believing that they are going to let their parents and families down, that they will disappoint them by being something other than what was wanted and expected. This is why it is so important for you to identify your loss, acknowledge your grief, and process it productively away from your child so that you can be present to support your kid authentically and without the disappointment they are likely so afraid of causing you.

Every person grieves in their own way and in their own time. Because coming out is a continuous ongoing process of discovery and identity development, you will likely find yourself confronted with revelations or realizations that trigger new and sometimes unexpected layers of grief throughout the coming-out journey. I can tell you from experience that this is not a simple process. It's not easy. It's unrealistic to expect that you are going to manage all these emotions gracefully and flawlessly without any stumbles or breakdowns. The emotions you're experiencing are happening in real time and you don't necessarily have the benefit of foresight or forethought. It is a complex and multi-layered process for you, your kid, and your whole family. Add to that further complications like religious beliefs, cultural expectations, socio-economic factors, family expectations, and community pressures related to the LGBTQIA+ experience, and the weight of your grief might start to feel overwhelming, resulting in trauma and isolation. This is why it is so important to identify and acknowledge your grief and its source as it's happening so you can find healthy ways to process it.

I want to pause for a moment and share with you why I feel this is one of the more important concepts we will explore together in this book. I have found that most parents of LGBTQIA+ kids want to do their best for their kids, but sometimes they end up sacrificing their own well-being in their attempt to be perfect parents. You may feel pressure to be the LGBTQIA+ champion in your kid's life, to be the cool parent who gets it and has no challenges with their kid's coming-out process. While those are admirable aspirations, you must also recognize that you are going through something intense right alongside your LGBTQIA+ child. It's an ongoing experience that's likely to be difficult and uncomfortable at times. The natural grief you are experiencing can compound that difficulty in unexpected ways that don't conform to logical thought or linear steps. That is why the self-care suggestions we've previously discussed are so important. You have to have space to take breaks along the way so you can reflect, process, and respond to your feelings productively. You have to give yourself permission to make mistakes and respond to them with forgiveness for yourself and patience for your kid. If you are in a marriage or partnership, you have to realize and acknowledge that your spouse or partner is also going through an intense grieving process that may be similar or different from the one you are going through. Make an active effort to connect with and support each other. Find ways to com municate and express your grief with each other in a respectful and honest manner. Feelings of isolation and abandonment are the most common roots of grief manifesting in destructive, hurtful behavior. Work to acknowledge, validate, and respect each other's grief as you focus on being there for your LGBTQIA+ kid.

As we've established, grief is a natural part of the human experience and a valid response to your kid's coming-out process. If you are grieving, here are some things you can do to help yourself and your family:

- *Attend support groups in your area:* Finding an LGBTQIA+-affirming parent group is vital for your well-being during this coming-out process. What's amazing about finding a group of parents who are on a similar journey supporting their LGBTQIA+ kids' coming-out process is that some people will be ahead of you on the path, others will be behind you, and some will be in the exact same place that you are. This shared experience is not only a great place to find resources but also a place to share your emotional experience in a compassionate and caring environment

- *Keep a journal:* Writing is cathartic for many! It allows you a quiet, private place where you can express your deepest, most intense feelings and not have to feel contained or constrained. As you are grieving the loss of your imagined child and embracing the potential of your very real LGBTQIA+ child, there are going to be feelings that come up that some might label as wrong or unsupportive. But if they are real for you, use your journaling time to wrestle your way through them and find a place of peace and release.

- *Work with an LGBTQIA+-affirming therapist:* If those feelings I mentioned above start to feel too big or unmanageable, immediately seek out an LGBTQIA+ trained, educated, and affirming therapist. They will have the knowledge and experience to help you process these intense feelings and access the love and support you have for your amazing and beautiful LGBTQIA+ child.

- *Eat well:* I know this sounds like a no brainer but whenever you are going through an intense emotional experience, including grief, your body is working really hard to balance all of the chemicals that are coursing through it. Over time, your grieving body will be functioning at a deficit and will need your attention so that you can heal and be emotionally present for you and your family. It is important to eat healthy foods and take supplements, if applicable.

- *Exercise:* No brainer number two. Intense emotional experiences take a toll on your body, and exercising is another tool to manage those huge emotional swings that your body is processing. Take walks or work out, jog or take a hike, work in the garden, or whatever exercise allows you to feel more at ease with your body and more centered in your emotional well-being. Even moderate physical exertion is a great stress reliever and may afford you some time alone to gather your thoughts in the process.
- *Get enough rest:* No brainer number three. Give yourself plenty of time to rest. Grief drains your emotional battery, and you will need to recharge more often. Listen to your body and give it time to heal and rest. Once recharged and rested, you will find yourself more emotionally available to your LGBTQIA+ child as they express more and more of their authentic identity.
- *Read and learn about the LGBTQIA+ community:* Knowledge is power and can assist you in regaining a sense of understanding over the experiences and environment you're traveling through with your LGBTQIA+ kid. It also helps reduce feelings of vulnerability. This book is just one step in your education as the parent of an LGBTQIA+ child, and I encourage you to seek out other sources of knowledge and education. Check out the Resources section at the back of this book as an initial guide to some quality resources. Some may be related to the coming-out process, while others may be learning about the vital and amazing LGBTQIA+ community that existed for generations just outside your usual scope of experience.

All these techniques can help you manage your journey through the grief process and gain a deeper understanding of yourself and your emotional response to your kid's coming out. And on the other side of this grieving process is the exaltation of embracing your LGBTQIA+ child's fully realized identity as you accompany them on their journey of growth, expansion, and exploration. By recognizing and embracing the grief process, inviting it in, allowing yourself to be informed and transformed by it, you will make yourself more available and enable yourself to be curious, optimistic, and excited about your kid's future.

Questions for contemplation

1. What was the vision of your kid's life that you developed over the course of their childhood?
2. How does it reflect on you that you attached so much meaning to that vision?
3. What are the most difficult parts of that vision to release?
4. Which of the techniques suggested for self-care feel right for you? Are there others you can add to this list?
5. Who can you speak openly with about these feelings of grief you are experiencing?

CHAPTER 7

Coming Out as a Family

I'm going to begin our discussion of family process by making an assumption. I'm going to assume that since you picked up this book and have invested time in reading multiple chapters on how best to support your LGBTQIA+ kid, that you are, in fact, here to actively support your kid through their coming-out journey. By making that commitment to support your kid, you are already way ahead of many parents of LGBTQIA+ children. What you may not have realized when you picked up this book, but are hopefully now starting to clue into, is that the coming-out process involves and affects the entire family. When a kid comes out to a parent as LGBTQIA+, it's natural for that parent's immediate focus to be on their LGBTQIA+ kid. But that coming-out moment is like a pebble dropping into a pond. The waves ripple outward affecting far more than just the impact point. Everyone in the immediate, and even extended, family is affected and will contribute to how things play out going forward. As much as you have been supporting and affirming your LGBTQIA+ child, you may also be discovering things, both positive and negative, about yourself, your family, your extended family, and your community at large, which may present you with the need to make difficult or complicated decisions.

Let's look at some of the effects and unexpected fallout from your LGBTQIA+ kid coming out, and I'll share some strategies for navigating this unfamiliar territory with the whole family in mind. One of the key concepts I promote in my work is that LGBT-QIA+ kids and their families often experience the best outcomes when parents/guardians support each other during their child's coming-out journey. Even the most loving and connected spouses, partners, and co-parents sometimes find themselves experiencing a complex and unexpected array of emotions and reactions to discovering their kid's LGBTQIA+ identity. Sometimes a parent's thoughts and feelings about their kid coming out don't line up with their own values and principles.

I often encounter parents who believe themselves to be open and accepting when the idea of LGBTQIA+ people is conceptual, hypothetical, or about someone else's kid. But when it suddenly hits home and it's their kid, they find themselves feeling things they don't want to face or admit. Sometimes parents, whether or not they are in a committed relationship with each other, find their thoughts and feelings about their kid's LGBTQIA+ identity don't align. If you and your spouse, partner, or co-parent(s) are reading this book simultaneously, you might have different takeaways or affinities with what you read, which might even lead to tension or conflict. One may read the discussion about grief and realize they have been obsessing over the "what did I do wrong" story, or worse yet, "what did *you* do wrong," while the other is stuck in the loss of the "dream" of who their kid would grow up to be. Then, when you attempt to initiate a conversation about your feelings and personal reflections on what you're reading, you realize that you're in different places emotionally or ideologically, perhaps feel frustration or resentment toward each other for focusing on or feeling what you think are the wrong things, and communication falls apart.

If you anticipate or encounter an experience like that, I

encourage you and your partner to read Chapter 8, "Time to Talk," and use the techniques I share there as a means of diffusing the charged emotions and searching out some common ground where you can understand, acknowledge, and eventually affirm where each of you is in processing your kid's LGBTQIA+ identity. I realize that parental relationships are complex and multi-faceted, and each one is unique. There may be many years and layers of historical baggage between parents that can make finding common ground and supporting each other difficult. But ultimately, *you* are the adults. *You* are the ones who bear responsibility for your kid's well-being, and it is *your* job to do what is necessary to protect, support, and affirm your LGBTQIA+ kid. If the bond between parents can stay strong and connected, there is a better chance that the coming-out journey will progress more smoothly for everyone in the family, and this united front will help all of you deal with challenges or obstacles that may present themselves from extended family, friends, or the wider community.

If you are a single parent, I encourage you to find support that can assist you not only in managing your personal feelings and reactions but also in paying attention to the needs of your entire family. Being a single parent is challenging enough by itself and when you add in the additional needs your children may express during the coming-out process, it can feel like too much to handle on your own. Seek out those in your extended family whom you can trust to be supportive and affirming of you and your child's coming-out journey. Ask them to be there for you, your kid, and the rest of your immediate family as much as they can while you are working through all the "ripples" that coming out has initiated. If you don't have someone like that to rely on (and even if you do), finding a local or online chapter of PFLAG can help you to get additional support from other parents who are on a similar journey and relieve you of the burden of having to go through this process all alone. Seek out ways to connect with local LGBTQIA+ organizations, resources, and events. It is important to know that you are not alone, and while these resources can be particularly helpful for single parents, they are also great for all parents.

Although your family's coming-out journey is initiated by your LGBTQIA+ kid, they aren't the only one having a coming-out experience. I encourage you to pay close attention to how the rest of the family is responding to this new knowledge and notice how your family dynamics might shift as a result. As your child comes out to siblings, they are in a vulnerable position. Your kid who is coming out may take on a heightened focus in the family but be aware that their siblings are also having strong feelings and reactions. They may have known about their sibling's LGBTQIA+ identity long before you or this may be new information for them as well. Take the time to check in with how they're doing and give them space to ask questions, share their stories, and explore their feelings. You may find your LGBTQIA+ kid's siblings reacting in unexpected and surprising ways. They may feel aggressively protective and supportive of their LGBTQIA+ sibling. They might also feel uninterested or ambivalent. They may be resentful of the extra attention their LGBTQIA+ sibling is receiving, resulting in tension or conflict between them, or a withdrawal of that child from their LGBTQIA+ sibling, and sometimes even their parents. They may have concern, anxiety, or even anger about the way their LGBTQIA+ sibling's identity may negatively affect their social standing at school and their relationships with friends and others in the community. One sibling coming out might even result in another sibling coming out in the same family. All these outcomes have the potential to put stress and strain on a family at this delicate time.

As I've noted several times throughout this book, communication is crucial, and this is a great moment to initiate conversations about gender identity and sexual orientation, encouraging the

entire family to become informed and educated, while also sharing their experiences and feelings around these complex concepts.
Perhaps there are aspects of themselves that your other children
want to share or explore. Family meetings and conversations don't
need to solely focus on your LGBTQIA+ child, and yet the topics of
gender identity and sexual orientation can be brought to the table
to expand everyone's understanding and personal relationship to
these larger concepts. Explorations of gendered roles in the family,
curiosities about personal expression, and questions about society's
messages about sexual orientation can all be valuable conversations
that encourage empathy and understanding, and ultimately lead
to support and affirmation.

While these initial conversations will usually involve your
immediate core family, there will be a point when it is appropriate,
and even necessary, for extended family to be aware of your kid's
LGBTQIA+ identity. If things have gone well with your immediate
family, you might feel anticipation and excitement, even eagerness
about telling extended family that you are the proud parent of
an LGBTQIA+ child. Your intentions behind sharing this news are
admirable and based on your strong feelings of pride, support, and
affirmation of your kid and their identity, and you want to bring
everyone you can into the circle of family love and support you
have started building. Perhaps you even envision a family gathering
to celebrate your LGBTQIA+ kid and the step they have taken by
coming out. Before you initiate these plans and communications,
please press pause! Take into consideration that while this news
affects your whole family, it is still your LGBTQIA+ kid's news, and
they likely have strong feelings you may not be able to anticipate
about who in the extended family gets to know now, who gets
to know later, and who may never get to know about their identity. As with your LGBTQIA+ kid's siblings, your spouse/partner/
co-parent(s), and even yourself, the reactions from your extended

family may be surprising or unexpected. Your LGBTQIA+ kid has likely given this a lot of thought before coming out and may know things about your extended family members' opinions and views that you are unaware of. I encourage you to discuss, understand, and respect your LGBTQIA+ kid's wishes and facilitate communication about them with your whole immediate family so you can present a united front when and if information about your kid's sexual orientation and/or gender identity is communicated beyond your immediate family unit.

I'd like to share an anecdote from my therapy practice to illustrate why it is important to give your LGBTQIA+ kid control over who knows about their sexual and gender identity, even when your desire to share stems from genuine support and affirmation. I was working with a transgender girl who was newly out to her family. She was struggling with establishing her new identity and crafting her visual presentation. She was exploring various looks and names, searching for what felt most authentic and resonant with who she was inside. As the Christmas holidays approached, her mom, in a well-meaning show of support, and without checking in advance, sent the entire extended family an invitation to a Christmas event using the affirmed name her trans daughter had been experimenting with, but hadn't yet decided to permanently adopt. My client was upset because she had not made a final decision on her affirmed name and felt locked into it because of her mother's hasty, though well-intentioned, actions. She was also afraid of her grandmother knowing and being upset by her expressed identity based on the culturally ingrained views and beliefs of her generation. She believed that the news of her transgender identity was likely to be confusing and upsetting to her grandmother based on previous interactions and experiences, and it was her intention never to tell her. The mother taking that decision out of her trans daughter's hands left the daughter feeling vulnerable, and lacking control of her identity and life. It left the mother feeling frustrated, and unappreciated for the support she thought she was giving her trans daughter.

As with most instances of family tension and conflict, the missing piece of the puzzle in this anecdote was communication. Any number of outcomes could have resulted from this mother and daughter simply talking about what approach should be taken with the invitation before it went out. Mother and daughter might have agreed that with the support of the family, it was worth taking the risk of letting the grandmother know about the daughter's trans identity and come up with a plan for handling any discomfort or conflict that arose. Or, they might have agreed it would be better to wait and find a way to word the invitation without a reference to my client's affirmed name. The point to take away from this example is that open and honest communication is the most effective tool you have in ensuring your LGBTQIA+ kid and your whole family are acknowledged, supported, and protected during the coming-out journey.

I've come back several times to the theme of communication throughout this book, but there is another recurring theme I want to reiterate, and that is forgiveness, and more specifically, forgiving yourself for the inevitable missteps and miscalculations that are bound to occur as you learn, explore, and discover alongside your LGBTQIA+ kid. Yes, in the example I just shared, the mom stumbled in her excitement to support her trans daughter, just like each and every one of us is going to stumble in our own efforts to provide support. I am a queer man whose career is based on working primarily with the LGBTQIA+ community and even I sometimes misjudge, miscalculate, and stumble. I am here to tell you, *it's okay*. As long as you acknowledge your mistakes, take responsibility, apologize, ask for education and clarification when necessary, and most importantly, *forgive yourself*, then you and your kid will get through these stumbles and continue moving along the path of understanding and connection you are working so hard on. As much as you want to be the perfect parent, there is no such thing. You are a human being with flaws and idiosyncrasies that will sometimes throw you off course and lead to mistakes. Keep breathing and be curious. You've got this.

Another place to follow your LGBTQIA+ child's lead is exploring their interest in connecting with LGBTQIA+-affirming organizations either in their school or in the community. Many schools have a GSA (Gay Straight Alliance), a QSA (Queer Straight Alliance), or other organizations that are affirming to all expressions of gender identity and sexual orientation. Although this may sound like an exciting prospect for your kid to engage with other LGBTQIA+ kids and allies, it is also a big moment for them and can bring up fears and concerns. If they choose to attend their school's version of QSA, the minute they walk through the door of that meeting, they have potentially outed themselves to the rest of the school. This can be a big step, even if they try to downplay their feelings about it. It can also impact your LGBTQIA+ kid's siblings who may go to the same school, so making sure everyone is on the same page before taking a step like this is important.

This same principle also applies to you and the rest of the family as you begin to connect with community resources. You will also be going through your own coming-out process if you choose to attend meetings and speak in these settings or publicly about LGBTQIA+ issues. You may run into friends who are kind and supportive of your journey, but you may also find that there are certain people in your life who will not be willing to support your journey of coming out with your LGBTQIA+ child. Just as your kid may lose some friends and encounter hostility when they come out, you may also lose some friendships and acquaintances who, for various reasons, cannot or will not join you in affirming and supporting the

LGBTQIA+ community, including your LGBTQIA+ child. Stand up for your child, yourself, and your family when they are mistreated and don't minimize the social pressure or bullying you may all face during these moments of coming out. These moments are going to sting and challenge your view of some of your relationships, and your community. Ultimately, I encourage you to prioritize the needs of your LGBTQIA+ child and your entire family over the small-minded views of ignorant, prejudiced people.

As you deepen your commitment to being an ally, not just for your LGBTQIA+ child but for all members of the LGBTQIA+ community, you and your family may find opportunities to become advocates and community educators. While this is not a role for everyone, it may feel right to put your energy toward educating the people in your circles when you are faced with slurs or jokes based on gender, gender identity, or sexual orientation, letting them know that such things are not tolerated and are not funny. You don't have to take on the role of the "tone police," but you can let people know the impact their words have and the pain that perpetuating LGBTQIA+ stereotypes and caricatures causes. Be willing to push back and educate people who make these types of slurs and jokes in person, on popular media, and these days especially on social media. One of the gentler phrases I use when first approaching someone who makes an offensive comment is, "I don't know if you are aware, but what you just said could be really hurtful to someone." For many people, this simple pointer toward awareness is enough to help them do better without aggressively shaming them. Finding your own way to handle these uncomfortable moments in a way that feels authentic to you can be valuable in maintaining the safety and well-being of your LGBTQIA+ child, while also making a bigger statement of support for marginalized communities.

Continue this support of marginalized communities as your family becomes more and more affirming by celebrating diversity in all forms. Encourage everyone in your family to discover and share a variety of books, movies, articles, and social media sites that positively represent and celebrate the LGBTQIA+ community. Explore and celebrate gender and sexual diversity within your family, your community, and around the world while acknowledging the bravery of people who stand up for the well-being of the LGBTQIA+ community.

I know this is all starting to sound a little grand and possibly overwhelming, so I want to return to the basics to ease your anxiety. Ultimately, the point of this discussion is to recognize that the coming-out process will have far-reaching and often unexpected consequences within your immediate family. Meeting them with a commitment to kindness, openness, curiosity, and self-reflection will result in more positive outcomes. Respect, clear communication, willingness to stumble, committing to forgiveness and picking yourself back up when you do, and, most importantly, loving each other as you travel this life-altering journey with your LGBTQIA+ kid all form the foundation on which your family will build its new authentic, supportive, and affirming dynamic.

As we bring this chapter to a close, I want to share one more anecdote from my work with LGBTQIA+ families, this one about a mother who stepped out of her comfort zone to support her LGBT-QIA+ kid and the important discovery she made as a result of their experience.

I had a client referred to me who had recently attempted to take his life. While in the hospital he was finally able to come out to his parents and tell them that he was gay. It was a painful, challenging moment for the entire family, but with education and knowledge, they quickly committed to building a supportive, loving, and affirming dynamic for their gay son. As my work with this young man progressed, he moved into the integration period of his coming-out process. He was out at school and started actively pursuing opportunities to become involved in the LGBTQIA+ community. He had one wish, though, that he was afraid to bring up to his family, which was that he wanted to go to the Pride celebration in his community. After some work to help him overcome his fears and anxiety about asking for this opportunity, he was finally able to express this desire to his family. His mom, whom we were concerned would not be receptive to the idea, surprised us all by volunteering to take him and be his chaperone to West Hollywood Pride. As the weekend approached and my client became more and more excited, his mom became more and more anxious. West Hollywood is one of the gay epicenters in America, and the West Hollywood Pride celebration is one of the oldest in the country. It's like diving into the deep end of the LGBTQIA+ experience, and way outside this mom's realm of experience and comfort. Despite all this, she kept her promise and they went to Pride. The car ride was tense as they both dealt with their nerves about what to expect when they got there. They ended up having a joyful, life-changing experience together that immeasurably strengthened their bond as mother and son, but also opened their eyes to the wealth of support and community that can exist among LGBTQIA+ populations. The experience had its intended effect as my client shared with me the overwhelming feeling of pride he felt being a part of this community. When I talked to his mom later, we processed her feelings after attending her first Pride event, which, while positive, were also a bit overwhelming. But her final and potentially most important discovery after attending Pride was, "I never realized there were so many hot men out there."

Questions for contemplation

1. How aware are you of how each of your family members is experiencing this coming-out process?

2. Are your spouse/partner/co-parent(s) and you aligned on how you are supporting the coming-out process for your LGBTQIA+ child? If not, what do you need to do to become aligned?

3. How can you initiate conversations with your family about the diversity of gender expression and sexual orientation?

4. How comfortable are you with openly supporting your LGBTQIA+ child and the community they are now a part of?

5. How will you respond to negative comments about your kid and the wider LGBTQIA+ community?

CHAPTER 8

Time to Talk

O ne of the challenges faced almost universally by parents, whether or not their kids are LGBTQIA+, is figuring out how to communicate with them. I work with parents all the time who complain about how closed off and distant their kids are, especially once puberty hits, and how frustrating it is to feel so disconnected and unsure of what's going on in their heads. Add to that the strain of your kid recognizing and embracing an LGBTQIA+ identity, then pile on the strain of coming out, and you can quickly feel as if you've been thrown in the deep end of the parenting pool without swimming lessons. That's why I am here to be your LGBTQIA+ lifeguard.

When I was working to become a professional therapist, a large part of my education and training was focused on learning and mastering an array of communication techniques and styles. I was also guided to hone my instincts and use all my observational senses to read between the lines and recognize the hidden doorways in my clients' mental and emotional walls. All that, coupled with my own lived experience as a queer person, gives me an advantage when I'm working with LGBTQIA+ kids. I frequently have parents tell me how astounded they are when they see their usually reticent and recalcitrant kid open up and talk more during an hour session with me than they have in a whole month at home. Well, it's easy for parents to feel frustrated and defeated after experiencing something like that but I'll tell you the same thing I tell those parents I work with in my practice. Give yourself a break and don't beat yourself up. There are techniques you can use to open up previously untapped lines of communication with your LGBTQIA+ kid and they are not difficult to master if you commit to being open, disciplined, and present. I am going to invite you behind the scenes and show you a powerful set of tools I use every day in my work that can help put you on a path to improved communication with your LGBTQIA+ kid.

When talking about issues of sexual orientation and gender identity with your kid, I encourage you first to consider their age and share information that feels appropriate for their developmental stage. When speaking with younger kids up to the age of five, conversations tend to be most effective when they are simple and concrete. Children at that age are generally very pragmatic and answers to their questions can be direct and simple. You usually won't need to provide expansive explanations with lots of detail and nuance. Addressing the specific facts they are curious about and leaving it there is usually the best approach at this age. Be affirming, supportive, and concise. There are many lovely age-appropriate books currently in print that can provide a helpful framework within which you and your young child can explore questions of gender identity and sexual orientation. These books can be used as conversation starters and will create an atmosphere in your household where young children know it is okay to be curious about these topics.

As your kid takes that big step out of the door into the school setting at around the age of six, they will be exposed to a new and unpredictable array of experiences and influences. At this age, your child's mind is like a sponge, soaking up and analyzing whatever information they come across. They will start making observations about their peers, other adults, and themselves, exploring much more deeply who they are and how they fit into a more socially complex world. They will quickly become more self-aware and more self-conscious. For young LGBTQIA+ kids, their observations and interactions with other kids, along with the attitudes and biases of the adults they are exposed to, will likely trigger questions about gender and sexual orientation that are more complex and specific than the ones you might have encountered with them before. The traditional social constructs that define gender identity in a strictly binary way and portray sexual orientation with a strictly heteronormative bias become more pronounced and influential in the school setting. This may lead to your child's first exposure to the cruelty of teasing and bullying, which they might experience directly, or witness as it is experienced by another child who doesn't fit the traditional mold. This is a time to listen not only to the questions that they ask and the observations they make but also to the feelings and unspoken questions that may be prompting those questions. How does it make them feel to hear bullying words on the playground and how do these words and attitudes affect them personally? At this age, kids are very aware of the messages around them regarding gender identity and sexual orientation, even if they don't yet understand the complexities and nuances of these subjects. They are likely to be more open to sharing their feelings and experiences if they trust that you, as their source of safety and security, will respond with support, curiosity, and understanding.

As kids cross the threshold into adolescence and face the inevitable tumult of puberty, their feelings become much more assertive and complex. For LGBTQIA+ kids, this often results in more overt expressions of their sexual and/or gender identity. This can be a particularly stressful time as their desire to be themselves and express their identity without restraint conflicts with their fears about fitting in, being accepted, compromising their personal safety, and being rejected by their family. It is common for LGBTQIA+ kids to use hypotheticals or take a roundabout path by asking for their parents' opinions about qualities or situations involving their friends, peers, strangers in public, or even people and situations in the media that relate to their own LGBTQIA+ identity as a means of testing the waters in their household. They often use this indirect probing to get a sense of what their parents' reaction might be to their own coming out. Remember, during these developmental stages, your kid's mind is still like a sponge, absorbing and processing the nuances of every reaction and response they encounter. This is the time when those observational instincts I mentioned earlier come into play. When you encounter questions like the ones I described above, learn to recognize them for the experiment they are and give your kid an outcome that ensures they know you will remain a source of safety, security, and love, not in spite of but because of their LGBTQIA+ identity, whenever they decide they are ready to share it with you.

As we've discussed, throughout your LGBTQIA+ kid's development they will be exposed to all kinds of messaging about sexuality and gender. The most powerful thing you can do as a parent is to normalize conversations about these messages and demonstrate that you have no negative or judgmental views or biases about the array of identities that are out there. Make it clear that even if you don't know everything there is to know about every identity in the LGBTQIA+ alphabet, you are eager to learn and understand. Look for opportunities to demonstrate your own journey of learning and discovery whenever you can. For example, when you are watching a movie with your kid and there is an LGBTQIA+ character or storyline, consider initiating a discussion with them about how authentic they think the representation and portrayal of an LGBTQIA+ character was. Let them be the teacher. Ask whether it fits with their experiences or those of their friends and peers. Perhaps share your observations about how these messages have shifted over time, explaining the shifts to your own understanding of the LGBTQIA+ experience now compared with when you were their age. Maybe even explore the generational messages that their grandparents were exposed to as well. It can be extremely powerful if these conversations also include any straight or cisgender siblings so that the diversity of gender identity and sexual orientation of your immediate family becomes a familiar and integral part of the family dynamic.

While these conversations can be incredibly powerful for both you and your LGBTQIA+ kid, I want you to understand that they may not always be one hundred percent comfortable for any of the parties involved. Communication takes a lot of effort and awareness. It is a skill set that requires conscious development. Most of us were not trained in anything but the most basic communication skills, which is why I'll reiterate my earlier suggestion to give yourself a break and don't beat yourself up. Effective communication takes practice, commitment, and time.

As I mentioned earlier in this chapter, I have the advantage of my therapist training and years of experience with hundreds of kids to assist me in getting these challenging conversations started. I am going to invite you behind the therapeutic curtain to learn some of the techniques that help me initiate and maintain open and meaningful conversations with LGBTQIA+ kids. These tips are not a magic wand and won't instantly transform patterns of communication that have developed between you and your kid over the course of your whole lives together. But with practice, commitment, and time, they will help you shift away from volatile, emotionally charged, or superficial interactions and move toward communication that is honest, affirming, and productive.

A great technique when talking to your LGBTQIA+ child is rather than asking them questions that can be easily answered with a "yes," "no," or the dreaded "fine," learn to ask what are known as open-ended questions or prompts. With this technique, a question such as, "How was your day?" becomes "Tell me about a challenging moment from your day" or, "What was a highlight of the day for you?" This style of question narrows the amount of information they need to process to provide an answer, while encouraging deeper contemplation. Often, an unexpectedly robust and insightful answer will pop out of your kid before they know it. These enhanced communications can then give you fodder for deepening follow-up questions and before you know it, you're having a beautiful in-depth conversation with your kid. Questions like, "What happened at school today?" can feel like witness chair interrogation that puts kids on the spot and instead of sifting through the wave of stimuli and experiences they faced at school to come up with an answer, they take the path of least resistance and say, "Nothing." Few things make a parent feel more disappointed and shut down. Narrowing the field of experiences they have to think about to come up with an answer for you can help steer them away from the default of shutting down the conversation.

Another effective technique that is related to open-ended questions and prompts is to begin by answering the question first, telling your kid something challenging you faced that day or sharing a highlight of your day. When you open the door first, making yourself vulnerable and sharing your own feelings and challenges, there is a good chance your kid will be more comfortable and open to responding in kind. It's not foolproof and it may not work every time, but it is one tool among many that can begin to break down the communication barriers you're facing.

In addition to open-ended questioning, you can also apply a skill know as paraphrasing. This is a technique where you repeat back to your kid what you believe you just heard but spoken in your own words. This approach allows you to make sure that you are accurately interpreting the information your kid is sharing with you. Then you ask them if you heard them correctly and allow space for them to correct you or clarify things. Here is an example of how this may look in practice:

> "What was your favorite moment from the dance tonight?"
> "I really liked it when the DJ played the song we requested, and I got to dance with all of my friends and we took over the dance floor."
> "Wow, it sounds like you and your friends had a great time dancing to your favorite song."

I know this all sounds rather simplistic, and that's the cool thing about effective communication: it can be simple. These simple conversations open up the gateway for deeper conversations when they are necessary, and they are much easier because you already have a bridge of communication built. In the above example, deepening questions might include, "Which friends were you dancing with tonight?" "Any of those friends someone you might be interested in?" "What would it be like to ask someone out at your school?"

An additional layer to this style of communication is known as reflective listening. What makes this a little different from paraphrasing is that you are trying to make the emotional content of the conversation a point of connection. In this technique, you will be asking them an open-ended question, listening to their answer, and then reflecting back to them the emotions you may have noticed while they were sharing their story. It might look something like this:

> "What was your favorite moment from the dance tonight?"
> "I really liked it when the DJ played the song we requested, and I got to dance with all of my friends and we took over the dance floor."

"That's sounds so freeing and joyful."

"It was, and it was also a little scary to be out in front of everyone."

This is how you find the feelings behind the words and move to an even deeper level. Of course, you are probably having trouble envisioning your LGBTQIA+ kid being this free and easy with their feelings, but you might be surprised at how much they actually want their feelings to be heard and acknowledged. The advantage of this technique is that if you can start by talking about how it felt to be free at a school dance, then when it comes time for more challenging conversations about coming out, you will have an emotional vocabulary already established with your child.

Where and when these conversations take place can also influence how open your kid is willing to be. Imagine you have had a long day at work with a million challenges popping up, emails flooding your inbox, and 12 business phone calls on your mind, and someone asks you how you are. The likelihood is that someone is about to get their head bitten off. Your kid is no different! Their school day is their work, and it is tough! I encourage all the parents I work with not to ask their kid how their day was the minute they jump in the car or come in through the front door. Give them some space and time to decompress. If you're in the car, let them have control over the music and be content driving home without a lot of chatter. When they walk into the house after a long day at school, give them some time to go to their room and just relax. Then, a little later, when their stress level has lowered, you can ease your way into a conversation using the techniques outlined above.

I also encourage parents to use an amazing and powerful technique that I like to call side-by-side conversations. I don't know if you have ever had this experience but imagine that someone sits down across from you unexpectedly and starts to ask deep, probing questions. My guess is that you would start to feel squirmy and anxious. It can feel as if they are staring you down and interrogating you. It doesn't make for the most effortless communication. In fact, it can often have the unintended effect of shutting you down. Instead, especially with LGBTQIA+ kids who may feel wary of being scrutinized and judged in their world, try this side-by-side approach.

As I mentioned above, getting kids to communicate is often easier when you avoid that witness stand interrogation feeling that many parents unwittingly default to. An example of how to easily execute the side-by-side conversation technique is to find a situation like taking the dog for a walk with your kid. Be willing to walk along in silence for a bit and then if you have a subject that you have been wanting to talk with your child about, ask a simple, low-stakes open-ended question. And then walk along in silence until your kid offers an answer. Don't press. Follow your dog's lead and simply pay attention to the world around you until your child speaks. Leave a little silence as you process their answer and then try a follow-up question or some reflective listening. Let the conversation unfold naturally and release any judgment about their answers or agenda of where you believe it should be headed. This is a key part of finding success with this technique. Your kid will sense if you're trying to lead or manipulate them into saying what you want to hear and if they do, they will likely shut down. Remaining neutral and unattached to the outcome of these conversations will start to develop trust between you and your kid. You'll probably be surprised by where your kid takes these conversations and learn more about them by simply being present and neutral. And what's great about this side-by-side approach, whether it's walking the dog, driving in the car, or making cookies together, the pressure to have a response is lessened dramatically for both parties and there is space to process on a deeper level. Sometimes in silence.

I bring up silence because getting comfortable with silence

is another valuable technique in your efforts to establish better communication. I know that concept seems counterintuitive, but it works. When you actively focus on developing comfort with silence, you create emotional space, removing the pressure and expectation for both your kid and you of always having to have a ready response. Have you ever experienced that mild feeling of dread in the pit of your stomach when you sense a conversation you are invested in is winding down and no new thread to keep it going presents itself? By cultivating ease with silence, you can train yourself out of that discomfort and change your perception of silence as a place of defeat to one of curiosity and possibility. This is not an easy skill to develop, and it takes time and practice, especially in a world that is filled with noise and stimulus, but it is worth the effort. Ultimately, making silence comfortable for both you and your kid can be another way of building trust and a feeling of safety and security for your kid. It is when kids feel safe that they are most likely to engage in meaningful, honest communication.

When using all these techniques, a powerful guiding principle is to let go of judgment. Your LGBTQIA+ child is going to potentially be sharing aspects of themselves that they are in fear of being judged for. Whether it is their feelings about themselves, their bodies, who they are attracted to, or even their LGBTQIA+ role models, they may struggle with real and intense feelings of shame, guilt, and self-loathing connected to these topics. And in a cisnormative heterocentric world they may find very little support for these conversation and curiosities in their daily experience. Make room in your heart and your mind to ease up on judgment, find a place of intellectual and emotional neutrality, and, letting your kid be the teacher, bring your own curiosity and openness to these conversations. Who knows, your LGBTQIA+ kid may wake up some topics that may be a point of personal growth for you even as you are offering your non-judgmental support to them. The great thing about these tools and techniques is that once you feel confident using them, they can then be applied to any situation or relationship in your life where you find communication to be challenging.

Questions for contemplation

1. Do you view yourself as a good communicator and listener?
2. Are there places where you could build and expand your skill set?
3. How often do you find yourself cast in the role of interrogator when trying to talk to your kid?
4. What are some creative and safe spaces you can cultivate to encourage open conversations with your LGBTQIA+ child?
5. Does judgment cloud your ability to communicate effectively with your LGBTQIA+ kid?

CHAPTER 9

The Big Talk

I hope after the previous chapter you feel that you have some solid tools and techniques that will help you communicate more openly and productively with your LGBTQIA+ kid. But you may have noticed, perhaps even with some sense of relief, that we have not yet addressed the biggest communication minefield that you, as a parent, are likely to face. You know what I'm talking about, and your fear and anxiety is already rising as we turn our attention to the elephant in the room. I'm talking about THE SEX TALK. Trust me, I know that this is one of the most challenging and uncomfortable topics to talk to your kid about. Despite that, it is an important conversation to have regardless of your kid's sexual or gender identity. Making sure your kid has a good shot at developing a positive and informed association with sex is one of the best gifts you can give them. It's an especially important thing for LGBTQIA+ kids, who may not have access to accurate and affirming information about the kinds of sex they will have, due to the education system's focus on binary, cisnormative, and heterocentric models of gender and sexuality. LGBTQIA+ kids are much more likely to enter the sexually active stage of their lives with negative associations, dangerous misconceptions, and misinformation about sex that can put both their emotional and physical health at risk.

I once heard someone compare the journey of self-realization LGBTQIA+ kids take toward coming out and developing as affirmed sexual beings to searching for a light switch, in the dark, in a room you've never been in before. Sometimes they'll trip over unforeseen obstacles and stub their toes or fall face first on the floor. There may even be people or situations that completely block their access to that light switch, and they may wander around in the dark all the way into adulthood. Of course, finding the light switch and turning on the light isn't the end of the road. It's just the act of revealing and illuminating their authentic sexual identity for themselves and everyone else to see.

For a straight, cisgender teen, the prospect of falling for someone they're attracted to and potentially hooking up comes with a normalized level of anxiety and uncertainty. In the cis/heteronormative home and school environments most kids grow up in, there are established avenues for them to manage their anxiety and address their fears, like talking to friends, siblings, or a trusted adult. School-based sex education is oriented toward their needs and desires, and popular and social media cater to their questions and curiosities. They generally don't have to worry about being ostracized or endangered when they communicate their sexual thoughts, desires, and questions.

For LGBTQIA+ adolescents, the stakes are higher and the dangers greater. Navigating that same anxiety and uncertainty can be a much riskier affair. Initiating and nurturing both romantic relationships and platonic friendships can be challenging and precarious. Communicating their sexual thoughts, desires, and questions to friends and peers can put LGBTQIA+ kids in a position of vulnerability that their straight/cisgender peers don't face and are unlikely to understand. Their biggest worry isn't just whether the object of their attraction will find them attractive, but whether that person is even capable of finding them attractive, and if they try to find out, will that person react with cruelty, aggression, or even violence? LGBTQIA+ kids will have seen first-hand the viciousness that their peers and even adults can direct toward them and other kids who don't fit the norm. The weight of the fear, anxiety, and uncertainty many LGBTQIA+ teens carry can become crippling if they don't have safe outlets where they can communicate about them.

Sometimes the simple process of getting ready for school each day can be a supreme act of courage for a teen who is facing intense feelings of isolation and fear. For those who have yet to come out, the secrecy they cling to can make those feelings even worse. Add to all that a romantic or sexual crush which an LGBTQIA+ teen can't safely pursue, and those feelings can be exacerbated to the point of emotional shutdown and potentially serious depression. As the parent of an LGBTQIA+ kid, it is important to recognize that knowledge, support, and comfort are like beams of a flashlight that may help to ease this journey through the dark as your teen works toward turning on the light switch.

Part of helping your kid through these difficult times means putting yourself in their place and working to understand what they're facing. Imagine walking around school and watching all your friends starting to date and having fledgling relationships that may include sex. There is someone you're attracted to as well, but you don't know if they might be attracted not just to you, but to your gender in general. You wear yourself out imagining the endless permutations of potential outcomes ranging from fairy-tale romance to humiliation and violence that could result from approaching the object of your attraction. Imagine that the body you were born in doesn't reflect who you are inside. Could the one you're attracted to look beyond the physical and see the real you? And if that happened, would they be willing to be open about having a relationship with you? If imagining this is stressing you out, then imagine what it's like for the LGBTQIA+ kids who are living this story day in and day out.

When it comes to education about their bodies and their attractions, most LGBTQIA+ kids are funneled into sex education classes where their teachers and textbooks fail to address their identities, feelings, behaviors, and experiences. Current research continues to show us the woeful lack of sex education programs that are inclusive of LGBTQIA+ sex positivity and information. This leaves many LGBTQIA+ kids without the knowledge and skills to initiate and maintain healthy relationships and protect themselves if they are engaging in sexual activity. This lack of affirming education has many repercussions for LGBTQIA+ kids, including having sex at an early age, having multiple partners, being more likely to have sex while under the influence of alcohol or other drugs, being more likely to experience dating violence, and being less likely to use condoms or birth control when they have sex.

What all this boils down to is the need for you as the parent of an LGBTQIA+ kid to start by educating yourself. Then get comfortable speaking openly about sex with your kid because they won't be getting the information they need from their school. It's important that you are willing to let go of preconceptions and misconceptions of what sex "should" be, while you let your ideas of what sex *can* be evolve and grow, helping you embrace and affirm the possibilities that will allow your LGBTQIA+ kid to have happy, satisfying, and fulfilling sexual and romantic relationships into their adulthood. This means you'll likely have to look beyond the cisgender heteronormative knowledge and perspectives that inform the basis for your own sexual and romantic experiences. Reading this book is a great start on your journey and I encourage you to seek out as many other great resources as you can find to give yourself the knowledge you need to be there for your LGBTQIA+ kid.

So, how does THE SEX TALK go down? Well, if your kid is already in their teens and has come out, you have some catching up to do. If not, and you think your kid may be LGBTQIA+ or questioning, just remember that it is never too early or too late to start communicating with them about their bodies and sex. Starting body-positive communication as early as possible with your kids can make the leap into open conversations about sex when they're older a little less intimidating and awkward. Young children will benefit from learning about their body parts and how they relate to them. Direct communication with young children about their bodies is necessary for several reasons. Having direct conversations with kids from three to nine years old will assist them in creating an age-appropriate vocabulary that supports body positivity and decreases any shame that they may be feeling about their bodies as they grow and develop. In addition, they will become more at ease with identifying when a part of their body hurts or feels uncomfortable. Finally, if children experience any inappropriate touch, they will have the language to describe what happened to them. Be aware that for transgender and non-binary youth, the success of these conversations hinges on having them in a context that supports and acknowledges their gender identity rather than their gender assigned at birth. Be open to questions and discussions about how their body parts may be different from kids whose gender identity matches their gender assigned at birth. This can be confusing and distressing for younger transgender kids, so making space for them to openly talk about the differences they are noticing between themselves and cisgender kids can help to lessen sensations of gender dysphoria and reduce stress and anxiety.

Each child is different and develops both physically and emotionally at their own pace. However, with kids entering puberty at younger and younger ages, I encourage parents to start talking with their kids about puberty and developing bodies at around nine years of age. Talk with them about the types of changes their body may go through as a means of demystifying this inevitable process. Ultimately, almost all bodies go through some form of puberty, and it is important for parents to help ensure that this natural process is not a surprise that catches kids off guard. Explain to your kids the kind of changes their body may go through and be sensitive to the possibility that your kid's gender identity may not match their physical body. Consider how these developmental changes may feel to a transgender child.

As puberty comes into full swing, conversations about sex are going to become more specific and this is where cultivating comfort with talking about bodies and sex early on is going to pay off in a big way. Now is the time to have deeper conversations about body parts, puberty, sexual orientation, gender identity, and sex. I know you may have trepidation about talking to your kid about sex, especially if this isn't territory you've covered with them in the past. But as someone who spends most of my professional life talking and working with teens, I can tell you with certainty that they are either having sex, thinking about having sex, contemplating why sex might not be for them, or sometimes a combination of all three. Talking to your kids openly about sex is not going to encourage them to have sex! Instead, it is going to prepare them to make intelligent and informed personal decisions about sex and their bodies based on facts and reality, rather than rumor and innuendo that they may find online or hear at school.

It is perhaps one of the great injustices in life that despite having gone through the trials of adolescence and puberty themselves, parents have so much trouble understanding and relating to their kids during those same developmental stages. Take a moment to pause and reflect on the intensity of your own puberty as a means to develop a little more empathy toward your beautiful LGBT-QIA+ kid's experience. From both a chemical and physiological standpoint, the changes that kids go through during puberty are intense. The impact of these changes is both physical, as their bodies develop and mature, and also neurological, as their emotions and urges develop and mature. As the parent of an LGBTQIA+ kid, it is helpful for you to know a little bit about their evolving neurobiology as a reminder that the changes you're seeing in their behavior aren't necessarily within their control. Increases in estrogen and testosterone at puberty literally change the structure of their brain, and along with it, the way your kid processes social situations and interactions. The hormones impacting their bodies prompt a proliferation of changes that suddenly increase feelings of self-consciousness, to the point where your child believes their behavior is the focus of everyone else's attention. This self-consciousness is often even more prominent in LGBTQIA+ kids, whose tendency to focus on what feels to them like a profound difference from their peers makes them hyperaware of every move they make and every word they say. They are often hypervigilant about any word or mannerism that might give away their gender identity and/or sexual orientation if they are not out. It can also result in erratic behavior when the strain of all that vigilance and control becomes too much, and they erupt with anger or rebellion. Understanding the effect these hormones are having on them can help you as a parent be less reactive to their behavior and more strategic about finding productive ways to understand, communicate with, and support them.

The other piece of developmental neurobiology that I feel every parent should be aware of is the huge differential in how the risk/reward response, which is intrinsically connected to their sexual impulses, develops in a teenage brain. You may start to see odd and erratic behavior from your kid and wonder why your teen seems incapable of thinking things through. You've likely found yourself wondering, "How did they ever think that was a good idea?"

One likely contributor is the fact that in the adolescent brain, the limbic system, which is the reward center of the brain, develops earlier and more quickly, while the frontal lobe, which is the impulse control center, develops later and more slowly. Research suggests that this is one reason why teens will often put themselves in risky situations without considering the consequences of their actions. The developmental imbalance I've described between the limbic system and the frontal lobe is also why making an active commitment to talking openly with your kids about sex is so important. Teens may literally be chemically incapable of stopping to consider how their actions might impact their lives and the life of those they are being intimate with when they are in a charged sexual situation. Having candid conversations about sex and how your kid wants to experience it *before* they are in a position to do so can result in better, safer decisions, rather than your kid trying to figure it out as they go when they're already in that sexually charged situation. Communicating with your kid so they understand the long-term consequences of their actions before they happen can go a long way toward setting them up for success when they find themselves in a situation where they actually have to make those decisions.

Let's shift our attention from the brain and move our focus toward the body. It is important to make your LGBTQIA+ kid aware that no two bodies are built exactly alike, genitally, or otherwise. That includes those of the same sex or people who identify as the same gender. During puberty, most kids experience a heightened awareness of their bodies and those of their peers. It is natural for them to start observing and making comparisons, including how their genitalia and visible secondary sex characteristics such as breasts, facial hair, Adam's apples, and pubic and other body hair compare with those of their peers. While this behavior is completely natural, it can be a source of confusion and discomfort for LGBTQIA+ kids, who may be overwhelmed and uncomfortable with the way their bodies are or aren't developing and their responses to the development they observe in their peers.

When I talk to the kids I work with about sex, I make it clear that I do not limit my definition of sex to penetrative intercourse. It's likely that there is a wide array of physically intimate acts that your kid and their peers may or may not define as "sex." As you communicate about sex with your kid, it's important to make sure you're on the same page and speaking the same language, which means establishing and understanding what constitutes sex for them. There is no right or wrong answer to what is or isn't sex. What is important is that you and your kid have a common frame of reference to talk clearly about the feelings and reactions that they are having toward sex as *they* define it. Your LGBTQIA+ kid's definition of sex could include activities like making out, kissing, stroking of body parts, masturbation (including mutual masturbation), frottage, oral sex, vaginal sex, anal sex, using sex toys (alone or with a partner), cybersex, and myriad other possibilities.

Are you freaking out? Does the thought of saying the words "anal sex" or "sex toys" to your kid tie your stomach in knots? Don't worry. That's a completely natural reaction and you're not alone. THE SEX TALK isn't easy. And the part they don't tell you when you become a parent is that it also isn't a one-time thing, at least not if it's going to do any good. It's an ongoing conversation which, to be effective, should develop and mature along with your kid. It is entirely likely that your kid will try and shut you down, close their eyes, cover their ears, and yell, "LA-LA-LA-LA-LA" to drown out the sound of your voice the moment you say the word "sex" to them. The discomfort for both you and your kid can feel monumental in the moment. This is the point when it's important to remember some of those communication tools and techniques I shared with you previously to help you ease into the conversation and work up to those gut-clenching words gradually.

As the old adage says, life is a journey, not a destination. Sexual stimulation and pleasure work the same way. And that journey can follow different paths for different people. Sex is physical and sensory, but also chemical, emotional, psychological, intellectual, social, and cultural. As a result, sexual exploration and discovery can be especially confusing and uncertain for LGBTQIA+ teens, who might be learning to explore the bodily sensations that work for them outside the prescribed boundaries of cisgender heteronormative practices and expectations. Committing to supporting your LGBTQIA+ kid during this period in their development is an important opportunity for you as both a parent and a human to grow and broaden your understanding of what sex and pleasure can be. Make a choice to suspend your attachment to ideas of good and bad, should and shouldn't, and gut reactions about what you would or wouldn't like. Instead, actively choose to remain neutral and open. Monitor your feelings so you can respond instead of react. Listen carefully to what your kid is willing and able to share with you, with the understanding that they may be exploring sex and bodies in ways that you may not have thought of. It's not a bad thing, just a difference of lived experience. Your LGBTQIA+ kid may find and embrace forms of stimulation that fulfill their desires and attractions in ways that are outside your understanding or experience. I encourage you not to make judgments or assumptions about how your LGBTQIA+ kid is or should be having sex. Instead, be open, curious, and observe as they explore and discover what satisfies their own personal needs, realizing that some of that process will involve trying things that teach them what they don't want in addition to what they do desire. And while those experiences may involve negative or uncomfortable feelings, they are not necessarily bad. They are part of the natural process of growing, learning, and maturing.

If you're reading this and continuing to wonder how in the

world you're supposed to bring this up with your kid in a way that won't end with both of you paralyzed with embarrassment, consider approaching the conversation from the angle of talking about safer sexual practices. This approach can be a win-win because it's an important part of what your kid needs to know about sex in general, but it can also be a way for you to bring up some of the sensitive and uncomfortable aspects of THE SEX TALK in a more hypothetical, less confrontational way that your kid may be less resistant to discussing. Of course, initiating a conversation about safer sex practices means you need to be informed and up to speed on what that actually means in this day and age. The way I like to start this conversation with teens is to tell them that when you have sex with someone, you are basically having sex with everyone they have previously engaged with sexually. This often gets a strong reaction from them and is one of the ways I circumvent that developmental disconnect I described earlier with their risk/reward response. The strong yet simple mental imagery which that metaphor creates seems to be very effective in putting their sexual decisions into a healthy perspective and encouraging them to look at the bigger picture. Once that happens, they tend to be much more open to talking about condom use, means of transmission for STIs (sexually transmitted infections), HIV, PrEP (pre-exposure prophylaxis, a pharmaceutical HIV preventative), pregnancy, and contraceptives, all of which should be at the core of any talk about safer sexual practices.

If your kids are sharing with you that they are sexually active, initial conversations can revolve around the basics of safer sex. These would include the consistent use of a barrier (condom, dental dam), having regular STI screenings, especially when initiating with a new partner, and paying close attention to their overall health and well-being. Although we might hope for this kind of awareness and responsibility in a perfect world, let your kid know that no one is perfect and the reason for bringing up the topic is to make sure they are aware and to encourage them to make the best choices they can. I talk openly with the teenagers I work with about how, although they may feel that they are well-informed about safer sexual practices, when the blood gets pumping and the hormones start raging it will be challenging to put on the brakes and take the precautions they know they should. The more prepared and knowledgeable they are, the more likely they are to make healthy, responsible choices.

Safer sex, though, is not just about the body. It is also about the heart, mind, and spirit. I believe it is vital to talk with kids, whether they are LGBTQIA+ or not, about the importance of intimacy and consent. When teens first explore sex, it is often a physical and biological journey, chasing what feels good and figuring out how to get more of it. Just like adults, some teens are more apt than others to connect sex and physical pleasure with emotions and interpersonal connection. For some kids, their sexual experiences will be much more profound on a physical level than an emotional one. For others, it will be the reverse. Sex and intimacy do not always go hand in hand, nor do they need to. Each person has to make their own decisions and come to their own conclusions about the role they want sex to play in their lives and the relationship they want it to have to intimacy. For some, that might mean using sex as an expression of love and commitment. For others, it might mean using sex as a form of recreation and physical release. Neither approach is intrinsically right or wrong, and some people may use a combination of both depending on the situation or their stage of life. It is important for teens who are becoming sexually active to examine what they want sex to mean for them in relation to both their physical and emotional needs. It may take experimentation for them to know what they actually want or don't want. What is important is for them to understand that those choices are theirs to make.

Regardless of your kid's perspective on what sex means to them, talking to them about the need to be respectful and aware of their partner's pleasure and boundaries, as well as their own, is key to helping them understand the responsibilities that come with the decision to become sexually active. Talk openly with your LGBTQIA+ kid about the importance of consent in any sexual encounter. In my work with teens, I define consent as an ongoing agreement between participants to engage in a sexual activity. It involves setting boundaries and expectations for everyone involved, including the understanding that those boundaries might change midstream and must be respected. An important aspect of consent is that agreeing to participate in something sexual doesn't mean consenting to participate in everything sexual. Encourage your kid to commit to checking in regularly to make sure everyone is still comfortable with what is happening. Establish a clear understanding with your kid that just because they feel attraction and desire, they can't assume that their partner feels the same desire and attraction, or that they will express theirs in the same way your kid might. Explain that they are not entitled to having their desire satisfied without understanding their partner's feelings and boundaries and receiving their consent beforehand. Conversely, also explain to your kid that they are not obligated to satisfy a sexual partner's desires just because they have placed themselves in a sexual situation, even if your kid initiated the sexual situation. Sex is a two-way street and so is consent. It needs to be both given and received for sex to be both physically and emotionally safe. I realize this can be another of those difficult and uncomfortable conversations but talking about consent with your LGBTQIA+ child will help keep them and their partners physically and emotionally safe. The ultimate goal of consent is to make a pleasurable and safe environment for sex to be free and enjoyable for all parties involved.

In my professional work with LGBTQIA+ teens, we explore how

transparency, vulnerability, trust, and communication are some of the key building blocks of intimacy in relationships. And while sex can be a way of deepening and strengthening the intimacy in these relationships, it is not a necessary ingredient for meaningful intimacy. Transparency and vulnerability are powerful bonding tools for creating intimacy because they require us to release the ego and expose the deeper feelings that are present, including the feelings that are pleasurable and connective as well as the feelings that may be difficult and distancing. As you communicate with your LGBTQIA+ child about the relationship between sex and intimacy, explore with them the idea that pursuing and cultivating intimacy with others, whether or not sex is involved, can help them to learn to love and understand themselves, while also building healthy relationships, whether they are platonic or sexual.

An aspect of your LGBTQIA+ child's sexual development that can be challenging for many parents is discovering that your kid is looking at porn. Access to pornography online is an unavoidable reality of the world we live in. Where in pre-internet days a kid (maybe even you) might have had a magazine hidden under a mattress, the internet contains a vast array of sexual imagery that can play both a positive and negative role in your kid's sexual development. The curiosity and arousal associated with pornography are not harmful in and of themselves. Combine these with the buffet of porn available at their fingertips and it's inevitable that they are going to take advantage of the opportunity to explore. This is especially true for LGBTQIA+ kids, who have much more limited access to information about the types of sex they want to have compared with straight kids. The internet, and specifically the porn it offers, can be a primary tool for them to understand the sexual mechanics and possibilities available to them.

What can be harmful is when pornography is interpreted as

a representation of reality. The context that many teens lack in understanding that porn is an expression of fantasy packaged as a commodity rather than a representation of reality can lead to the development of unhealthy ideas and expectations. I encourage you to talk openly about it with your kid and help them to put what they are viewing into context. Help them to understand that porn is a business and what they are seeing is not a realistic view of sex. It is staged for camera, and carefully orchestrated and edited. It is often intercourse-centric, focusing on mutual climax, and the performers are frequently portrayed as stereotypical caricatures who represent hyper-idealized sexual roles and idealized, often exaggerated body types. Let your teen know that it is not bad or morally wrong to view and even enjoy pornography but help them understand that sex in real life isn't like sex in porn. If they don't see themselves reflected in the porn that is accessible to them, it can be beneficial and productive to discuss how that may feel as well.

I hope you are still breathing and taking this all in with an open mind. I know these conversations about sex can be challenging, but as a parent it is also important for you to explore your own comfort with talking openly about sex and noticing any biases toward cis/heteronormative constructs that could interfere with an in-depth conversation with your LGBTQIA+ kid. Many parents find it challenging to bring conversations of sex into the house and will often wait for a perfect moment to present itself rather than being proactive in initiating the conversation. Instead, think of sex education as an ongoing conversation where setting a foundation of comfort early can allow for a steady deepening of supporting the needs of sexually active LGBTQIA+ adolescents. Be willing to listen to your kid's experience, coach and educate them when necessary, and provide candid and objective feedback about risks they may be exposing themselves to in their search for sexual expression.

Questions for contemplation

1. What are your own biases and agendas surrounding sex?
2. How might they interfere with talking openly about sex with your LGBTQIA+ kid?
3. How do you define sex?
4. What are your personal feelings about pornography and how might those feelings interfere with having a frank conversation with your LGBTQIA+ child?
5. What is your personal relationship with consent and how can you explore that with your LGBTQIA+ kid?

Final note!

Many of these tips and techniques about talking openly about sex could be used with all your kids and maybe even your own partner!

CHAPTER 10

Love, Life, the Pursuit of Happiness, and Beyond

Before we dive into our discussion of romantic relationships, I want to take a moment to commend you for making it through the sex chapter (you did read the SEX chapter, right? No cheating!) and sticking around to continue our exploration of the best ways to support your LGBTQIA+ kid. GO YOU!

It's important to reiterate that most parents find talking to their kids about sex to be one of the most challenging and anxiety-inducing responsibilities they face. But as we've discussed, the benefits, especially for LGBTQIA+ kids, of making sure they understand the joys and possibilities, as well as the risks and responsibilities, of exploring sex can't be overstated. Now, however, we'll turn our attention to romantic relationships, a topic that is closely related to sex, but which might feel a little less daunting to talk about with your LGBTQIA+ kid. The fact is that teenage romantic relationships are fraught at the best of times. Throw in the added complexity of LGBTQIA+ identities and they can turn into a minefield, both for your kid and for you as a parent who loves and wants to support them. As with sex, there are numerous potential obstacles that can arise for LGBTQIA+ kids that don't necessarily exist or aren't as intense for their straight cis peers. Discovering, facing, and navigating those obstacles can be frustrating, discouraging, and frightening. It can also result in periods of low self-esteem, depression, and feelings of resentment, awkwardness, hopelessness, and isolation. Again, establishing open lines of communication with your LGBTQIA+ kid becomes more important than ever when sex and relationships come into play because these are the experiences and challenges they will likely be the most reticent about. It will require patience, creativity, insight, and persistence for you to keep productive communication going and provide the support that they may simultaneously want and resist.

There is one truth that applies universally to all relationships. Regardless of whether they are romantic or platonic, adult or adolescent, involve LGBTQIA+ identities or not, healthy relationships take work. And healthy romantic relationships take extra hard work. There is a strong narrative of fairy-tale love and "happily ever after" that holds a pervasive storyline in our culture. It shows up all over the place in the way romantic love is portrayed in movies, television, books, and other media that kids are exposed to. While those traditional romantic constructs aren't intrinsically bad, if they're not given proper context they can set the stage for unrealistic expectations and aspirations that your kid and any romantic partners they may have can't live up to. Now, you might be thinking that the disillusionment and disappointment that goes along with learning that real-life romantic relationships don't follow the fairy-tale tropes is just part of growing up, something we all go through, and you'd be right. But for LGBTQIA+ kids, their journey of growth and discovery is already tougher and more perilous than what their straight cis peers face. Giving your LGBTQIA+ kid as much insight and guidance as possible about what real romantic relationships are and what they take to maintain is one way you as a supportive parent can help them avoid some of the relationship landmines they are bound to face.

There are lots of ingredients needed for a romantic relationship to form. While those ingredients differ from person to person, they often include things like physical attraction, sexual chemistry, emotional connection, intellectual connection, shared interests, shared experiences, and a host of other affinities. But while the presence of one or more of these ingredients may set the stage for a romantic relationship to form, they are rarely enough to sustain it on their own in the long term. When the topic of relationships comes up in my work with LGBTQIA+ teens and their parents, I often encourage them to start by taking the LGBTQIA+ variable out of the equation for a moment and approach the discussion from a purely human perspective. I ask them to come up with what they believe the key ingredients are for having a positive romantic relationship. Then we talk about what the people in the relationship have to do to make it work going forward, once the ingredients are in place. This can be a helpful exercise since most LGBTQIA+ kids don't get to see many relationships like the ones they will have seen depicted in popular media. Once they have ideas about what any person might need to have a successful romantic relationship, we then consider what someone with the kid's sexual and/or gender identity might face in their relationships so that both the kid and their parents begin to understand the opportunities, possibilities, and challenges that may lie ahead. I encourage you to try a similar approach with your LGBTQIA+ kid. Talk with them to get a sense of what they believe romantic relationships are and aren't. Discuss what they take to maintain. Perhaps share some experiences from your own life to illustrate your perspective on what they are for you. Kids often think adults have everything figured out and that the answers to life's questions are black and white, all or nothing. Sometimes sharing your own uncertainties, vulnerability, and imperfections can make your kid feel more comfortable in lowering their barriers and opening up to you.

As you begin to initiate these conversations with your LGBTQIA+

kid, it will help you to have an idea about some of the most common challenges they're likely to face before you start. Oftentimes, the biggest (and occasionally insurmountable) challenge is for one LGBTQIA+ kid to meet another LGBTQIA+ kid who has a compatible sexual/gender identity. In the school environment, there is a limited number of LGBTQIA+ kids, and an even smaller number of those who are comfortable being out. Because of this, the pool of potential dating partners can be miniscule, if it exists at all. Your kid may feel attraction toward another kid at their school, but that attraction may not be reciprocated. While this is something every kid faces regardless of their sexual orientation or gender identity, it can be devastating when a kid realizes that the vast majority of people they may be attracted to not only don't but can't reciprocate their attraction. It can be even more crushing if it turns out that the object of a kid's attraction has a compatible sexual and/or gender identity but the attraction is still unreciprocated.

Circumstances like these can leave LGBTQIA+ kids feeling discouraged and hopeless, which can then lead to reckless and unhealthy choices and behaviors. When these devastating moments arise—and they will—you are probably going to experience your own struggles with feelings of powerlessness and the realization that this isn't something you can fix for your kid. The most important thing you can do is simply be there for them. Put your focus on providing a non-judgmental space for your kid to unload the pain and disappointment they are feeling. They may not be willing or able to communicate with you about it but do what you can to let them know that what they're feeling is real and valid. Let them know that while you haven't gone through what they're experiencing, you understand that what they're facing is hard and uncomfortable. Although you may not feel the same attractions as your LGBTQIA+ kid, try to remember the pain and discomfort of high school dating and empathize with your kid about their challenges.

We have all been there in one way or another and although the attractions and rejections may be different, the feelings that accompany them are universal.

While we just painted a fairly bleak picture of the dating pool for LGBTQIA+ kids in school, that doesn't mean it's impossible for your kid to find compatible romantic partners. Let's say your LGBTQIA+ kid is developing a healthy romantic relationship with a partner(s) who appreciates them for exactly who they are. If you haven't done so already, this fledgling relationship presents a prime opportunity for you to initiate a conversation like the one I described earlier about what it takes to build and sustain a strong relationship. While your conversations about sex will involve a lot of the more uncomfortable things like body parts, STIs, and consent, your conversations about romantic relationships will be more nuanced. If you take sex out of the equation, helping your kid understand what makes a real romantic relationship really boils down to defining intimacy and helping your kid understand its role in their relationship. Certainly, sex and physical stimulation can be exhilarating, but sharing with your kid about the additional layers of connection intimacy offers can assist them in building more rewarding and longer lasting relationships. For as little information as there is for LGBTQIA+ kids about the mechanics of sex, there's even less when it comes to addressing how to develop intimacy in a relationship. As we discussed earlier, sex and intimacy are not mutually inclusive or exclusive, and depending on the circumstances your kid is facing, your conversations may touch on one or the other, or both. When a romantic relationship comes into play for your LGBTQIA+ kid, it offers a great opportunity to tie all these concepts together. This is when you can explain the importance and power of intimacy in sustaining and cementing a romantic relationship, as well as the role sex can play in deepening it. When I work with LGBTQIA+ kids, I describe intimacy as a bond based on one or more of five main components, including emotional, intellectual, spiritual, experiential, and physical connection. Here I've shared the definitions I use for each of these components in the hope it will help you when you discuss intimacy with your LGBTQIA+ teen.

Emotional intimacy is a state of trust in which romantic partners share their authentic emotional truth in an unfiltered and reciprocal way without risk of judgment or rejection. There is enormous power in being able to share your deepest feelings, insecurities, and dreams without fear. For LGBTQIA+ kids, a connection like this can be particularly profound since they face so much risk of being ostracized for the feelings that come most naturally to them.

Physical intimacy is the use of touch and physical sensation to demonstrate and enhance a connection between romantic partners. While people often associate physical intimacy with sex, and more specifically, the pursuit of orgasm, in the context of intimacy it involves much more than that. Since most teens are a walking stew of bubbling hormones, sex is naturally going to be a big focus for them, but it is only one of many ways to create physical intimacy. Sometimes more casual types of contact like kissing, caressing, cuddling, massaging, or handholding can be the most powerful ways of cultivating intimacy. The context in which these types of contact occur can also intensify their effect. For example, the simple act of handholding in public can hold profound meaning for LGBTQIA+ people, since it can represent not only a demonstration of attraction and connection between romantic partners but also a shared declaration of defiance, pride, and solidarity against society's disapproval of LGBTQIA+ relationships.

Intellectual intimacy is the exhilarating affinity romantic partners share around the alignment and interplay of their ideas, viewpoints, philosophies, and beliefs. And while alignment of ideas is often a key driver of attraction, sometimes that affinity and interplay is expressed through healthy debate and disagreement. In healthy relationships, the commitment to mutual respect of ideas and beliefs ensures that the opposition enhances rather than strains the romantic connection. The ability to disagree safely and respectfully is a necessary component of stable and mature romantic bonds.

Spiritual intimacy can produce an exhilarating affinity between romantic partners in the same way that intellectual intimacy can. Spiritual intimacy is the alignment and interplay of spiritual beliefs, viewpoints, and feelings between romantic partners. Let your LGBTQIA+ kid know that sharing their spiritual beliefs or lack thereof is another effective yet often overlooked means to connect in relationships.

Experiential intimacy is the affinity that exists between romantic partners based on their mutual interest and participation in activities, hobbies, and pursuit of shared experiences. Sometimes these affinities can develop along the way as one partner introduces the other(s) in the relationship to experiences they didn't know they would like, while other times, the connection can be based on a partner indulging in something they don't necessarily enjoy because they know it is important and/or meaningful to another partner. Over the course of a relationship, the memories of these shared experiences become part of the bedrock of the romantic connection.

While all these expressions of intimacy are instrumental in helping your LGBTQIA+ teen build deeper connections with their romantic partners, they can also help them outside the romantic context as they strive to develop bonds with friends and family. Developing intimacy is just as important in platonic friendships and relationships as it is in romantic ones. Taking these concepts to heart might also end up helping you deepen the intimacy in your own relationships.

Earlier on, I mentioned that healthy relationships take work, and healthy romantic relationships take extra hard work. This is true of any relationship regardless of the sexual orientation and gender identities of those involved. However, it is often especially important for LGBTQIA+ people to put in the extra work because our relationships are often subject to strains and scrutiny that straight cisgender people don't experience. Through the course of my work as a therapist working with kids, adults, and couples, I have identified five particular areas of focus that can help anyone, but particularly LGBTQIA+ folks, build and maintain healthy, lasting relationships. While these suggestions don't cover everything that's needed to build a stable, fulfilling relationship, they address the most common pitfalls that can lead to discord, strain, and, ultimately, the loss of intimacy and collapse of the relationship.

Practice clean, clear, and connective communication: It's no secret that communication is a necessity for any healthy relationship. The ability to have candid conversations in which romantic partners can express their feelings and needs in a safe, respectful space is one way to ensure that the seemingly small and inconsequential challenges and obstacles that naturally arise over the course of a relationship don't fester over time and turn into irreparable wounds. This doesn't mean that every conversation has to be a deep dive into the minutiae of the relationship. Instead, it means that when there is a need to address a problem or concern, there is a safe space for romantic partners to be honest and vulnerable. The trust that this type of communication builds over the course of a relationship will lay the foundation for stability and longevity.

Embrace romantic partners for who they are: This is a reciprocal affirmation where each person in the relationship feels confident and secure in who they are without the need to conform to a standard set by their partner(s). This doesn't mean that romantic partners don't continue striving to grow, mature, and develop as individuals and human beings. It also doesn't mean that romantic partners don't address behaviors that may be hurtful or counterproductive to the relationship. It means that the fundamental components that define each partner's personality and identity are embraced, respected, and valued in the relationship. Accomplishing this can be challenging and confusing for any adolescent, but especially for LGBTQIA+ teens, who often struggle with the process of self-discovery that leads to understanding and revealing their authentic identity. The culturally entrenched fairy-tale influences that we discussed earlier can also sometimes complicate things if teens go into a relationship holding themselves and/or their partner(s) to unrealistic and unachievable standards and expectations. Encouraging LGBTQIA+ teens to understand the importance of embracing their romantic partner(s) for who and where they are can help them avoid some of the pain and disillusionment they might otherwise face as they attempt their first romantic relationships.

A necessary level of compatibility must exist: There are all sorts of characteristics and affinities that make romantic partners compatible. They are often difficult, if not impossible, to predict and quantify, but they have to be there in order for a romantic relationship to survive. Sometimes a relationship will thrive because "opposites attract" and romantic partners balance each other's strengths and weaknesses. In other situations, partners are compatible because their personalities and identities are similar, allowing their lives to seamlessly mesh. The presence of compatibility is closely tied to the ability to develop and sustain intimacy as we discussed earlier, since without it there is no common ground on which to build a relationship.

Romantic partners are still independent people: A lot of people I work with find themselves hampered in their relationships because they fall into the "you complete me" dynamic, which ultimately boils down to unhealthy co-dependence, and is often another symptom of an attachment to fairy-tale concepts of love and relationships. Real-life romantic relationships have the best chance of success and longevity when the participants love, support, and complement each other, while still maintaining their own authentic individual interests, pursuits, and identities. Ideally, rather than having romantic partners who are incomplete without each other, you have independent, complete, yet connected individuals who, by coming together in a romantic relationship, create and nurture something greater than themselves.

Love oneself while loving one's partner(s): Oscar Wilde once wrote that "to love oneself is the beginning of a lifelong romance." While Wilde's words were colored by the subtext of his own tragic relationship woes as a queer man in a hostile society, the essence of his sentiment holds true today. Similar to maintaining independence and individuality in a relationship as we discussed above, it is also crucial for romantic partners to maintain self-love, self-esteem, and self-affirmation for their own identity. It can be easy to fall into relying on a romantic partner to provide validation and affirmation. But doing so leaves the relationship vulnerable to slipping into unhealthy co-dependence where rather than being focused on what each partner is bringing to the relationship, the focus is on what they are taking from it, resulting in insecurity and the negative kind of neediness that repels intimacy and trust.

Now, you may be thinking that these are some pretty heavy and mature relationship concepts to be expecting teenagers to master, and you'd be right. The key here isn't preparing or expecting your LGBTQIA+ kid and their fledgling romantic partner(s) to get all this right on the first try. The aim is to give your kid an idea of what healthy, mature romantic relationships look and feel like, as well as what it takes to build and maintain them. Just like we all did, they will make all kinds of mistakes and fumble all over themselves as they experiment and explore their own attempts at starting relationships. The concepts and suggestions I've shared above are meant to help you give your LGBTQIA+ kid a head start on forming an aspirational picture of what their future relationships can be. This isn't meant to put pressure on you or your LGBTQIA+ kid to have perfect relationships. On the contrary, these suggestions are meant to give you and your kid the tools to face all the imperfections and obstacles that life and love will inevitably throw in your path.

I'm sure you've noticed by now that throughout this chapter when I have referred to an LGBTQIA+ teen's potential romantic partner(s), I have done so in both the singular and plural. As the supportive and affirming parent of an LGBTQIA+ kid, it's important for you to be aware that the sexual orientation and/or gender identity of your kid and their romantic partner(s) isn't the only way in which their relationships might look different from the cis/heteronormative model of relationships you were raised with. It is possible that your LGBTQIA+ kid might embrace something other than the dyadic formula you have taken for granted as the proper or standard model for romantic relationships.

A form of relationship building that is important for you to be aware of is polyamory, which refers to people who have multiple consensual romantic relationships at the same time. Polyamorous people have multiple loving, intentional, and intimate relationships at the same time, usually with all partners being aware of the others involved in the relationship. In one version of polyamory, the multiple partners are all involved with each other simultaneously, while in another, one individual may have relationships with multiple partners who are not romantically involved with each other but are aware of each other. There are also those who have more than one romantic relationship simultaneously, and while everyone involved is aware that this is or could be happening, they do not know or discuss the other partners. While your reaction to your kid engaging in this kind of relationship dynamic might range from cautious acceptance to deep discomfort, polyamory is more prevalent than you may imagine among both straight and LGBTQIA+ populations. It is also becoming more and more common among teenagers, even if they aren't necessarily open about it, as a means to find a supportive, loving, and connected tribe. The key concepts in polyamorous relationships are that the partners have open communication and create mutually agreed on guidelines that dictate the structure and dynamic of the relationships. As with any romantic relationship, communication is the key to success, and that is more important than ever when the number of people participating in the relationship grows.

If your kid is in a polyamorous relationship and they choose to share it with you, I urge you to take a moment to breathe, listen, and absorb what your kid is telling you. Return to that affirming approach we've discussed where you approach your kid from a place of neutrality and let them be the teacher. Your kid is probably not looking for your approval of their relationship but will be watching for signals as to whether you are disappointed, disgusted, or judging them. They will use their impressions to determine whether they can speak openly about it with you and hopefully garner your support and understanding. As you are learning about this relationship style, remember that polyamorous relationships can be complex as the partners navigate through the emotional territory that comes up when multiple people are involved. It takes a lot of conscious effort to establish the guidelines that are the cornerstone of making a polyamorous relationship work, and your ability to be present with your LGBTQIA+ teenager as they navigate this landscape creates the safe space they may need to explore their feelings.

Earlier in this book we discussed many of the numerous sexual and gender identities that the LGBTQIA+ alphabet encompasses. Two of the identities we have not yet discussed in detail are asexual and aromantic. It is important for you to be aware of these identities since the same coming-out journey of discovery applies to them as it does to being gay, lesbian, bisexual, transgender, or any other queer identity. As we learned earlier, asexual people typically experience very little to no sexual attraction or arousal toward others or themselves. While puberty and adolescence awaken sexual attraction and the drive to have sex in kids who are not asexual, those who are do not experience that arousal response. Asexual people's response to sex and attraction can range from ambivalence to disgust and may change and evolve over the course of a person's life. Asexuality differs from celibacy in that celibacy is a choice to not act on sexual arousal, while an asexual person may not actually have a sexual arousal response to act on. You may hear your LGBTQIA+ kid use the word asexual but more commonly they will use words like "ace," "aces," or "A" in describing themselves.

I encourage you to keep yourself open to the concept that asexuality means different things to different kids and the nuances of identifying as asexual can be fluid. Try not to make assumptions about what your child's asexuality means. Instead, let them share with you as they feel comfortable about this aspect of who they are. It's okay to ask them questions but don't pressure them or allow them to feel obligated to educate you. They may still be exploring what asexuality means to them and not feel comfortable attempting to give concrete answers regarding a still-formulating identity.

Let your LGBTQIA+ child know that what they are sharing with you doesn't alter your love for them and that you are willing to do your best to listen and learn along with them.

There are nuances that exist under the umbrella of asexual identities. One of these is demisexual, which is a person who experiences sexual attraction and arousal only when a deep emotional connection has been established with another person. These are people who develop sexual attractions primarily in the context of a deep, ongoing relationship, which can suddenly become romantic when the sexual attraction and arousal surface. Demisexual people can be any sexual orientation. Demisexuality doesn't dictate the gender, gender identity, or gender expression of the object of a demisexual person's attraction. It is not unusual for an individual to believe they are asexual, only to find themselves experiencing strong sexual impulses toward someone after achieving a deeper level of emotional intimacy than they have experienced before. At that point, the individual may decide they are demisexual rather than asexual and go on to have an active and fulfilling sexual relationship with their partner(s).

Another nuanced identity that falls on the spectrum of asexuality is greysexual, also known as "grey-A" and "grey-ace." This is a person who rarely experiences sexual attraction or may have a low interest in exploring sexual desire. This low interest may apply to partnered sex as well as solo sex and they may not prioritize sexual attraction when choosing a potential partner(s). This does not mean that they will not share affection, and will often express this through cuddling, sleeping together, and talking. They can feel completely fulfilled by these activities and not need to pursue a sexual relationship.

You may feel slightly uncomfortable assimilating these valid identities as your LGBTQIA+ child shares them with you, but I encourage you to recognize the courage it took for them to do so.

In a world where the stories of sex can feel omnipresent, many kids who fall on the asexual spectrum can feel as if they are broken or dysfunctional. Seeing their peers seemingly obsessed with sex while they feel little or nothing can be an incredibly frightening and isolating experience. Asexual kids often experience fears about spending their lives alone, being unlovable and unattractive. It can be a huge relief to your child to feel your love and affirmation as they share and explore their identity with your support.

The final identity that is becoming more and more widely understood is being aromantic. An aromantic person is someone who may feel sexual arousal and attraction toward others and with themselves but has little or no romantic attraction to others. An aromantic person may not experience feelings of romantic attraction and doesn't feel the need to be in a romantic relationship to feel complete. They may not experience romantic crushes or have the desire to connect on a romantic level with sexual partners. Understand that your aromantic child can still have intense loving feelings and long-term relationships. They just aren't romantic in nature. They can form powerful emotional connections with people and express empathy and love for friends, family, pets, and others. Aromantic people often feel negative social pressure to be in romantic relationships, to find the right person and "settle down." It is important to understand that aromantic people are not "commitment-phobes," selfish, or sex-aholics. They simply do not find fulfillment and connection through romantic relationships. Some additional nuanced definitions in the aromantic spectrum include: greyromantic, a person who experiences romantic attraction infrequently; and demiromantic, a person who experiences romantic attraction infrequently and only after developing a strong emotional connection with someone.

Asexual and aromantic identities are not mutually inclusive or exclusive. A person can be one or the other, or both. If your kid comes out as asexual or aromantic or a combination, I encourage you to meet your kid where they are at and learn from them how these identities influence the way they walk through the world.

There is a strong possibility that if your LGBTQIA+ kid is in a romantic relationship, then they will likely experience the pain and hurt of a breakup at some point. While this is something that most kids who explore romantic relationships in their teens will go through, the added pressures and scrutiny that LGBTQIA+ kids are under can make breakups harder than usual. It's not easy to see your kid in pain, but your support during this difficult time can go a long way toward helping them heal after the end of a relationship. I encourage you to remember your early dating life and find empathy for what your kid is experiencing. With that empathy in place, remember that each person experiences a breakup in their own way. Sometimes the easiest way to support your LGBTQIA+ kid is to ask them what they need and then give it to them. They may be able to tell you, or they may just need a hug and a good cry. Be aware that small moments of connection and support go a long way for a kid who feels lost in the heartbreak of a relationship ending. With the advantage of age and perspective, you probably know that their pain is just part of growing up and that it will burn bright, then fade as they move on with their life. But remember that your kid doesn't have the benefit of your wisdom. Minimizing their feelings or suggesting that they are being overly dramatic can erode the trust you're working to build and close down the lines of communication you are trying to open. Let your kid feel their feelings and reassure them that they are real and valid. They are going to get a lot of advice and direction from their friends. You can create a different level of support that allows them to just feel what they are feeling without having to have a plan of action attached to their healing process. Give them time and space to travel through those feelings as they make sense of their loss and initiate the process of putting themselves back together once the heartache starts to ease. And a bowl of ice cream doesn't hurt either!

I hope that through the course of this chapter you have discovered the myriad ways that people can develop relationships or not, and that this knowledge will allow you to travel this journey more successfully with your LGBTQIA+ child. Regardless of the relationship model that ends up feeling right and natural for your kid to pursue, the important thing is that they feel loved, fulfilled, and supported, both by their romantic partners and by you. As you continue to grow, learn, and adapt in your understanding of your LGBTQIA+ kid's journey, you will begin to notice the connections that will increase your ability to support and affirm them for exactly who they are and the relationships that feel authentic for them.

Questions for contemplation

1. What are your biggest fears about your LGBTQIA+ child getting into a relationship?
2. What are those fears based on and would they be the same if your child was cisgender and heteronormative?
3. What are your personal guideposts when identifying a healthy relationship?
4. What feelings arise when you contemplate that your kid may be asexual?
5. How would you best support your LGBTQIA+ kid during a breakup?

Final note!

Many of these tips and techniques for talking openly about romance and intimacy could be used with all your kids and maybe even your own partner!

CHAPTER 11

When the Real World Gets in Your Way

I am going to continue in this chapter with the ongoing assumption that you have made it this far because you truly want to understand, support, and affirm your LGBTQIA+ kid. Understanding, support, affirmation, and, ultimately, love, are what every kid, regardless of their gender or sexual identity, deserves from their parents, but it is even more important for LGBTQIA+ kids due to the biases, ignorance, prejudices, and bigotry they inevitably face in our society. Decades of research show the extent to which proactive parental support helps LGBTQIA+ kids in their emotional, mental, intellectual, and physical development and well-being. Instances of depression, self-harm, and suicide are dramatically lower for LGBTQIA+ kids from families where they are affirmed and embraced. LGBTQIA+ kids from supportive and affirming families are often also better equipped to confront, endure, and manage hostility and bullying that occurs outside their family.

Unfortunately, it doesn't take much to find the evidence that many LGBTQIA+ kids are not the recipients of parental and familial support and affirmation. In some families, not everyone is aligned in their values and beliefs, which can result in tension and conflict when a kid in the family comes out, not only between parents and their LGBTQIA+ kid but also between parents, and between other members of the immediate family, as well as extended family members. In these instances, providing the necessary understanding, support, and affirmation for your LGBTQIA+ kid can be complicated, challenging, and in some of the worst scenarios, dangerous. In this chapter, we'll look at some of the possible obstacles and challenges parents might face in their efforts to be there for their LGBTQIA+ child and explore some potential strategies and solutions for overcoming them.

Rejection from within the family

We've established that LGBTQIA+ kids face a lot of negativity, obstacles, and challenges in our society. The sources of those vary widely and can include classmates, teammates, coaches, teachers, religious leaders, politicians, social media, mainstream media, and even strangers. The negative messages and influences can be direct or peripheral, or both. But the most damaging and painful source is when hostility and rejection originate from within a kid's own family, and especially from a parent. One of the difficult aspects of my work with adolescents is seeing, time and again, the detrimental long-term effects of the pain caused when they are rejected simply for being who they are by those who should be their primary advocates and protectors. I've lost count of the number of kids who have ended up in my office because the pain of living their truth or hiding who they are from their unsupportive and non-affirming families became so intense that they believed the only option available was to kill themselves. Think about that for a moment. These beautiful, vibrant, unique, and vulnerable young people, 12, 13, 14, 15 years old, with limitless potential and their whole lives ahead of them, are so wounded by the pain of rejection, or even the expectation of it, that the only solution they can see is death. That is how powerful and basic the need for parental support and affirmation is for kids, and especially for LGBTQIA+ kids. The same research that shows the positive long-term effects that understanding, support, and affirmation have on development and well-being for LGBTQIA+ kids also shows the extent to which their absence dramatically increases the risk for mental, emotional, and physical challenges, including depression, anxiety, alcohol and drug overuse, eating disorders, negative or risky sexual experiences and behaviors, self-harm, runaway/homelessness, and suicide.

As we continue, remember I am following my assumption that you are a parent who is invested in and committed to understanding, supporting, and affirming your LGBTQIA+ kid in their coming-out process and their LGBTQIA+ identity. Unfortunately, it is discouragingly common for parents and other family members to have differing values and beliefs when it comes to sexual orientation and gender identity. These differences often become problematic, leading to tension and conflict when they negatively influence how the family unit reacts and responds to an LGBTQIA+ kid coming out. These differences can start off as subtle biases that lie beneath the surface, then manifest suddenly, and in some cases unexpectedly, when one or both parents are confronted with the reality that their kid is LGBTQIA+. But in some families, the biases are not subtle and take the form of overt hostility, disdain, and outright bigotry toward LGBTQIA+ people. A family that unanimously shares those attitudes can be a worst-case scenario for an LGBTQIA+ kid, making the idea of coming to terms with their authentic identity and coming out feel impossible, often with tragic results.

If you are a parent of an LGBTQIA+ kid but your spouse/partner/ co-parent(s) is not understanding, supportive, and affirming, you may be reading this book in secret, being careful and subtle with your words and actions as you try to apply some of the supportive principles and techniques I have been sharing with you to give your kid some semblance of support. Perhaps your kid's other parent is not even aware of their LGBTQIA+ identity, which you are keeping secret, fearing their negative reaction. Perhaps your spouse/partner/ co-parent(s) is conflicted and unsure of their ability to support and react positively toward your child's coming-out journey and you want to shield your kid from feeling "less than." These are complex and painful challenges that can undermine the stability of a family and have lifelong consequences. But ultimately, your LGBTQIA+ kid's mental, emotional, and physical well-being must take priority as you decide how to protect your kid from anti-LGBTQIA+ sentiments and hostility within your immediate family, which can include any or all of the following:

- Verbal harassment
- Physical harassment
- Telling an LGBTQIA+ kid that God will punish them
- Blocking access to LGBTQIA+-affirming resources
- Forcing a kid to act more "masculine" or "feminine"
- Excluding an LGBTQIA+ kid from family events
- Isolating an LGBTQIA+ kid from their supportive and affirming friend group.

These negative behaviors and reactions and others like them are NEVER acceptable. Please remember that your kid's safety is always a first priority. Understand that a rejection of your LGBTQIA+ child's authentic identity, particularly from within their family, damages their sense of identity, undermines their self-worth and self-esteem, and isolates them from the family unit. If these types of harmful behaviors are showing up in your household, it may be best to find an alternative living arrangement to keep your LGBTQIA+ kid safe and healthy. If your spouse/partner/co-parent(s) is unable to join you in affirming and supporting your LGBTQIA+ child and reacts with anger, fear, violence, or disgust when they learn about their child's sexual orientation and/or gender identity, I encourage you to take action to keep your kid safe rather than risking their well-being as well as your own. This is not an easy path to take, and as I indicated earlier, could have lifelong consequences and implications, but it is essential to ensure that your LGBTQIA+ kid has a safe and stable living space while family dynamics are addressed, and you assess whether it is possible to overcome the obstacles your family is facing that are preventing an LGBTQIA+-affirming environment.

One of the most dangerous and pernicious reactions families, and especially parents, can have to their kid coming out is to pressure their child to "change" their gender identity or sexual orientation—sometimes through a program specially aimed at doing this. These attempts at so-called "conversion therapy" are often pursued by parents with a misguided belief that they are helping their LGBTQIA+ child toward a better and healthier future, that they are giving them a chance to be "normal." Some of the current names this process may be masquerading as include:

- Reparative therapy
- Conversion therapy
- Sexual orientation change efforts (SOCE)
- Sexual reorientation efforts
- Sexual attraction fluidity exploration in therapy (SAFE-T)
- Ex-gay ministry
- Eliminating, reducing, or decreasing frequency or intensity of unwanted same-sex attraction (SSA)
- Promoting healthy sexuality
- Sexual addictions and disorders counseling
- Sexuality counseling.

In reality, these programs, under any name, are exposing LGBTQIA+ people to cruel and damaging practices that attack and ravage core aspects of their identity with devastating emotional, physical, and psychological results. Often underlying these abusive attempts at conversion is a belief that LGBTQIA+ identities are a mental illness or disorder, an assumption that is not based on any medical or scientific evidence. If you or your spouse are considering any of these sexual orientation change efforts (SOCE), I implore you to stop. All leading professional medical and mental health associations reject "conversion therapy" as a legitimate or safe medical treatment. These practices cause significant psychological distress and damage and can result in depression, anxiety, lowered self-esteem, internalized LGBTQIA+-phobia, self-blame, post-traumatic stress disorder, sexual dysfunction, and suicide. LGBTQIA+ people who have been exposed to these types of abusive treatment also experience significant social and interpersonal harm, loneliness, social isolation, difficulty with intimate relationships, and loss of social support systems. No matter what your beliefs or feelings are about your LGBTQIA+ child's identity, I once again urge you to stop, and examine the research and evidence that overwhelmingly demonstrates not only the impossibility of changing a person's sexual or gender identity but also the devastating harm caused by attempts to do so.

Religious influences

The majority of programs purporting to administer so-called "conversion therapy" have arisen out of religious groups and organizations. It is no secret that most organized religions with widespread influence in our society have a historical tradition of disdain, hostility, and oppression toward LGBTQIA+ people and identities. While we have seen notable moves among some religious communities to shift their ideologies and embrace LGBTQIA+ people in recent decades, attachment to long-standing religious beliefs, influences, and affiliations remains one of the most common sources of strain and conflict within families confronted with an LGBTQIA+ family member coming out. Just like the cultural constructs dictating gender roles and behaviors we discussed at the beginning of this book, which are ingrained from our earliest moments of life, religious indoctrination is something that also frequently happens very early on in a person's development, becoming part of the foundation of their world view. Challenging those ingrained ideas and beliefs can cause intense emotional reactions ranging from disappointment to betrayal to disgust, horror, and even rage. For an LGBTQIA+ kid, witnessing a parent having those emotions and knowing they are the reason their parent is feeling those things is a traumatic experience of rejection from which many LGBTQIA+ people struggle their whole lives to heal.

Many LGBTQIA+ kids who come from homes with strong religious influences find themselves trying to navigate a minefield of reconciling the religious beliefs they've been taught with the reality of their emerging LGBTQIA+ identity. There is an intense dissonance that many LGBTQIA+ kids who grow up with anti-LGBTQIA+ religious influences experience between what they have been told they should feel and believe and what their bodies, hearts, and minds are telling them is true and authentic for them. This dissonance often results in constant, grating, low-level stress and anxiety that grows over time and can be responsible for a host of physical and psychological consequences such as hypertension, depression, and suicidal ideations. For some LGBTQIA+ kids, the stress and anxiety caused by the dissonance they are experiencing can become so omnipresent that they start to feel "normal," supplanting their connection to feelings like contentment, confidence, and comfort. It is common for LGBTQIA+ kids to bargain with God, agreeing to give up things or people they love if God will only "fix" them. This sets up a destructive cycle of commitment and failure that can devastate an LGBTQIA+ kid's self-esteem and self-worth, becoming another consequence that many LGBTQIA+ people spend years of their lives working to unravel and heal.

Many parents of LGBTQIA+ kids, who have never experienced a crisis of faith or been confronted with a reason to question the religious teachings they subscribe to, find themselves confused and overwhelmed by the dilemma they face trying to reconcile the love they have for their LGBTQIA+ child with their commitment to the tenets of their faith. If this is part of your experience as the parent of an LGBTQIA+ kid, I encourage you to approach your feelings with the same compassion and lack of judgment I've encouraged you to show to your kid. Acknowledge that this is uncharted territory and you aren't going to come up with all the answers overnight. You may find yourself searching for support within your religious community. Based on what you encounter, you may find the support you need, or you may arrive at the conclusion that you and your family need to explore other paths of spiritual fulfillment. You might even find yourself becoming an advocate for change and progress within your community of faith. Whatever you encounter, I encourage you to reject any advice or suggestions from your support network, religious/spiritual or not, that encourage you to shun or change your LGBTQIA+ kid. There is no course of action involving rejection of your child and their identity that will result in a healthy or positive outcome for you, your family, or your LGBTQIA+ kid.

I respectfully suggest that the opinions of your priest, pastor, imam, rabbi, or other clergy, as well as those of your religious study group, friends, and extended family, while valid and important, have less weight than your commitment and responsibility to love, nurture, protect, and affirm the radiant, vulnerable young being whose future health and well-being is in your hands. There is a powerful technique that I have seen help parents of LGBTQIA+ kids time and again when issues of faith become an impediment to creating a supportive and affirming family environment. Your religious community is likely going to have lots of opinions and feelings about the LGBTQIA+ community. Some or all of them may be biased generalizations and based on ignorance, propaganda, misinformation, or political agendas, using fear as a motivator. Their influence can be confusing and disconcerting. Rather than internalizing those voices and their messages, make an intentional effort to check in with yourself. Find a quiet place where you won't be interrupted. Find your spiritual center and focus on your personal relationship with the god or higher power you are connected to. Send a prayer out to the god you have lived your life with and ask what they want for you and your kid. Ask for guidance about what you need to do and who you need to be for your LGBTQIA+ kid. Almost every person that I have encouraged to adopt this practice has come back with the answer—their god simply wants them to love their child as they are. The simplicity of that answer is both affirming and comforting for parents and often paves the way for them to affirm and love their child during the coming-out process and beyond.

Rejection from extended family

Whether or not religious influences come into play within your family, you may find that there is a lack of support for your LGBTQIA+ kid among your extended family. You may have built a beautiful affirming atmosphere in your household, but when you interact with grandparents, aunts, uncles, cousins, and other extended family members, there may be resistance or even hostility toward your LGBTQIA+ kid. Grandma may not understand the practice of using your transgender kid's affirmed pronouns or name. An uncle may express disgust at your lesbian daughter bringing her girlfriend to Thanksgiving dinner. A cousin might decide to take a stand that your bisexual son is just confused and needs to choose one team or the other. Any or all these scenarios could play out depending on the family dynamics and personalities we have inherited. Introducing LGBTQIA+ family members into the mix is one of the quickest ways to make the Norman Rockwell family portrait start to crack. The thing to remember is that your immediate family unit, with whom you have created an affirming, supportive dynamic, doesn't have to crack under the pressure just because members of your extended family aren't doing their part. Bringing a united, informed, compassionate front to extended family gatherings can often defuse potentially uncomfortable moments that arise. Family gatherings can be stressful but if you all work together, you can create a net of safety for your LGBTQIA+ kid and your immediate family unit.

To create this united front within your family, I encourage you all to communicate as a family unit before you attend an extended family gathering. Make a conscious commitment as a family to prioritize and protect each other first. Identify extended family members, situations, and scenarios based on your prior experience which could be hurtful or harmful to your LGBTQIA+ kid and the rest of your immediate family unit. Strategize about ways to avoid or diffuse those individuals and situations. Bullies often operate by isolating the object of their aggression and cruelty so discuss ways to ensure that no one in your immediate family unit becomes separated from their support network during the visit or event. Enlist the help and support of any trusted extended family members or friends who are committed to supporting and affirming your LGBTQIA+ kid and your family unit. Generally, bullies are cowards and will back off when they meet the open resistance of a united family front.

Discuss how open your LGBTQIA+ child wishes to be about their identity and how they feel you can best support them. Follow their lead to collaborate on an approach that feels safe for them and doesn't put pressure on the rest of the immediate family to figure things out on their own. Ensure that siblings are on board and committed to supporting and respecting their LGBTQIA+ sibling's plan. These types of conversations can establish the conventions and agreements that will make your LGBTQIA+ child feel empowered and alleviate stress and anxiety for everyone else. An example of one of these mutually negotiated rules would be that "we don't force or challenge grandma to use my affirmed pronouns." Remember that your LGBTQIA+ kid is taking the lead in collaborating on these rules. It's also important to remember that as your LGBTQIA+ kid grows, develops, and matures, their needs and those rules may change and evolve, perhaps multiple times.

One useful technique you can employ ahead of the family gathering that can provide an additional safety net is to create a safe word that your LGBTQIA+ kid or anyone else in your family unit can use to signal that they are feeling pressured and uncomfortable. This mutually agreed on word or phrase is your clue that your kid needs a little assistance. Oftentimes, the best way to provide that assistance is to go outside or somewhere private, creating some separation and space to decompress. A little time away from the uncomfortable family moment can give your kid a chance to breathe, reset, and disengage from the emotional charge of the triggering moment.

Rejection from the community

Another source of obstacles and challenges that may emerge as you work to be an ally and advocate to your LGBTQIA+ kid is the community you live in. Living in a small, tightknit community can be a wonderful way to grow up. There are lots of benefits to that classic small-town atmosphere, where everyone knows everyone and people look out for and support each other. On the flip side, small-town communities can also be judgmental, homogeneous, and suspicious or even hostile toward non-conformity. This can be confining for an LGBTQIA+ kid who is discovering their identity but might not be ready to be the center of attention because of who they are. In small communities, it is often the case that everybody knows everybody's business and secrets are hard to keep. There is also likely to be less diversity in small towns and communities, which means fewer LGBTQIA+ people, fewer role models, confidants, romantic partners, and resources for LGBTQIA+ kids who are trying to figure things out.

For a kid who is ready, willing, and able to come out, the scrutiny of a small-town community may make them feel as if they are under a microscope and every move they make toward creating their affirmed identity will be examined, discussed, and in some cases ridiculed and condemned. For a kid who is struggling with coming out, that scrutiny may be too oppressive and they will continue to hide their authentic LGBTQIA+ identity for years, often until they move away. Many LGBTQIA+ kids who grow up in small towns believe that moving away is the only option if they want to find happiness and fulfillment in their lives. As a queer man who lives in a large city, I have a certain sense of protection and freedom to live an openly queer life. It is easier to discover and connect with people with whom I have things in common, and that journey of coming out can often be experienced with a certain level of anonymity, or at least without notoriety. As a parent, you may also discover that many of the resources that I am referring you to as a means of finding support just don't exist in your small town. In cases like this, you may have to be more creative and resourceful in finding support and may have to travel to access LGBTQIA+-affirming resources for both you and your child.

To counteract the dynamic that is often present in smaller communities, you may need to take on the role of advocate (with your kid's input and blessing) to be a catalyst for change in your community. If you find that your kid's school is not creating a safe environment for your LGBTQIA+ child, you may need to challenge the status quo and advocate that they bring in resources, whether they are books, trainings, or consultants, to educate the educators and build a more affirming school environment. While there will likely be some resistance to bringing in these types of outside resources, as a provider who offers these services myself, I find that these types of educational trainings can be a productive means of initiating institutional change. As part of my work, I regularly speak with and train school nurses on how to create LGBTQIA+-affirming practices in their schools. What I find is that after some initial distrust and anxiety, usually based on ignorance, insecurity, and misinformation rather than bigotry or animosity, most school personnel want to provide a supportive experience for *all* the kids at their schools, including those with LGBTQIA+ identities.

Another approach to diffusing anti-LGBTQIA+ sentiment in smaller communities is to focus on community-building efforts that can bring together people of differing viewpoints and lived experience. This might include organized LGBTQIA+-affirming events at community centers, informal gatherings at barbecues and in backyards, or extended conversations with local leaders in your area to expand their knowledge and views regarding LGBTQIA+ people and especially LGBTQIA+ youth.

Sometimes, though, there may be so much community resistance to supporting the LGBTQIA+ community that you and your family will need to have deep conversations about how best to keep your LGBTQIA+ child safe. This may mean finding supportive resources online for you and your child, planning trips to larger urban centers focused on accessing LGBTQIA+ care for your kid, or even contemplating if the town you live in can support your needs as a family going forward. A change in your family's location or your LGBTQIA+ kid's living situation may be the best way to offer them a safe and supportive environment. This last approach may sound drastic but forcing an LGBTQIA+ kid to remain in an abusive environment where they are endangered by the very people charged with protecting them can have a lasting negative impact on their mental, emotional, and physical health.

These and other obstacles may show up throughout your journey to being an understanding, supportive, and affirming parent to your LGBTQIA+ child. These moments can feel overwhelming and, as we are often discovering on this journey, they will challenge many of your core beliefs and even lifelong relationships. Just as your child is coming out and growing into their affirmed identity, you are growing and changing as well. Sometimes those changes in you are going to feel smooth and authentic. At other times they will feel scratchy and suffocating. Change is never easy but as you move through and learn from the obstacles you encounter on this journey, you may be surprised at the beautiful, powerful, and radiant person that you now see looking back at you in the mirror.

Questions for contemplation

1. Are you and your partner aligned in how affirming you can be toward your LGBTQIA+ child?

2. How do you imagine your extended family's ability to support your LGBTQIA+ child?

3. Are there certain family members whom you can identify as being more supportive, others as less? How will you connect with them?

4. How do your spiritual/religious beliefs align with your support of your LGBTQIA+ kid?

5. Are there steps you need to take to encourage your community to become more LGBTQIA+ affirming?

CHAPTER 12

So, You Want to Be an Advocate

Having arrived at this point in our journey of learning how best to understand, support, and affirm your LGBTQIA+ kid in their coming-out process, you've likely experienced a gamut of emotions and reactions to what can certainly be an overwhelming amount of information, techniques, and advice. I trust that, by now, you're feeling better informed about the best ways to support your LGBT-QIA+ kid during their coming-out process and although there are still many questions and challenges that will arise, you are starting to feel more secure and confident in your knowledge, awareness, and capability. You might even become more confident in your power as an agent of productive change and influence in both your LGBTQIA+ kid's life and also in your wider community. It's natural that even with all this additional knowledge you still have feelings of anxiety, uncertainty, and fear about what your LGBTQIA+ kid will experience when they walk out of the front door and face the opportunities and dangers the world will present to them. As a parent, you naturally want to make sure your LGBTQIA+ kid is safe and supported. With so many unknowns in the world you may feel as if you want to step up and be a proactive advocate not only for your child's well-being but the well-being of all LGBTQIA+ kids. As you become cognizant of all the daily challenges LGBTQIA+ kids face you may feel fired up and angry. You may want to march into their school and shake things up. You might want to testify at government hearings to advocate for policy changes to protect not just your own but all LGBTQIA+ kids. You might feel ready to march in a Pride parade and shout to the world that LGBTQIA+ kids are a beautiful, irreplaceable part of our society.

Let's press PAUSE. As resolved and energized as you may feel, I want to invite you to reflect on what it would mean to become a public advocate for the rights of LGBTQIA+ kids and how it might affect the people in your life, including your own LGBTQIA+ kid. Moving into advocacy is a courageous and vital pursuit that can be a catalyst for productive change and progress on both a local and worldwide level. At the same time, advocacy can require a commitment of focus, time, and attention that can become all-consuming. The work to be done will never end and the need for people to do it will never lessen. It is important to consider where your time, energy, and focus will do the most good throughout the stages of growth and development for your LGBTQIA+ kid and your family.

In the earlier stages of your LGBTQIA+ kid's coming-out process, it may be more beneficial for you to direct your energy and focus toward them and their immediate needs rather than on the needs of the wider community. Becoming a loud and proud voice for LGBTQIA+ rights while your kid is still finding their feet and coming to terms with their own identity might put a spotlight on them that they are not ready for. It could end up outing your LGBTQIA+ kid in environments where they are not currently open about their LGBTQIA+ identity. It could also have implications for your kid's peer group and their social circle if you find yourself in adversarial situations with other parents or administrative bodies in your kid's school and community.

If you are feeling the pull to become a budding LGBTQIA+ advocate, I encourage you to have your first discussions with your LGBTQIA+ kid. Share with them your ideas and plans for stepping out in a more public way to advocate for LGBTQIA+ rights. My experience in the overwhelming majority of situations I have observed among my therapy clients and their families is that most kids will have an initial negative response to a parent's blossoming public advocacy role and will need time to process their feelings about it. Give them some time and space to embrace your new passion. Discuss the boundaries and parameters for your advocacy that would make them feel more comfortable. Let them know what your future goals are and what you hope to accomplish in your efforts so they know what to expect moving forward and can incorporate that knowledge into their own plans and decisions. By committing to ongoing communication and collaboration, over time you will be able to forge a path that feels comfortable for both of you. They may even start to feel pride in the fact that you, as their parent, want to become an active participant in their world and embrace their LGBTQIA+ identity on a proactive, meaningful level.

As I have mentioned in earlier chapters, a great place for you to find support for yourself and your family during the coming-out process is to join a local group for parents of LGBTQIA+ children. This is also a great place to get your feet wet in learning how you can step up your game to become a community advocate for your LGBTQIA+ kid. With all the unknowns that you are facing with your LGBTQIA+ child, the parents you will meet in these groups can be a wonderful resource and support network who can help address your fears and anxieties. They are also people who may have begun the journey into advocacy and activism themselves and can give you advice about where to take your first steps.

For most parents, those first steps involve becoming more aware of school policies concerning and addressing the needs of LGBTQIA+

students and understanding how those policies are implemented in their kid's school. School is the biggest part of any kid's daily life, and feeling safe, secure, and respected at school by both their peers and the faculty who is responsible for them is important for any child but especially LGBTQIA+ kids. According to various studies, among LGBTQIA+ youth in schools, nearly 60 percent say that they feel unsafe in their schools simply because of their sexual orientation, while almost 45 percent say they feel unsafe because of their gender expression. All the LGBTQIA+ kids I work with share accounts of being bullied both verbally and physically in school and feeling that there is no one at school who can or will help them. Although many schools purport to have policies in place to keep LGBTQIA+ kids safe, those policies often only pay lip service to satisfy state or local mandates and are not actively implemented. The kids know this, both the bullies and those they bully. Be aware that the bullying can come not just from students but from teachers and staff as well.

This gap between policy and implementation might be a worthwhile starting point for your advocacy journey. You have every right as a parent to approach your school and learn first-hand about their policies and response procedures for instances of harassment and discrimination toward LGBTQIA+ students. Meet with as many school faculty and staff members as you can access to discuss issues like LGBTQIA+ safety, anti-discrimination, and inclusive curricula on campus and work with them to help expand those policies and approaches. At first you may experience resistance, but I encourage you to be persistent and seek out allies as they present themselves within the school. Work together with them to make your school a safer place for all LGBTQIA+ kids. As your advocate voice becomes stronger, it is to be hoped that other parents, faculty, administration, and staff members who are committed to creating safe spaces for LGBTQIA+ students will feel empowered to speak up and join you in working toward change. Most often, school administrators hear from parents who want to limit the visibility and rights of LGBTQIA+ students, so it's even more important for all parents who support LGBTQIA+ youth to make sure their voices are heard and respected. Speak up and challenge discriminatory or stereotyped statements at gatherings like PTA meetings, school events, and parents' nights.

You can also assist your school in creating a GSA (Gay Straight Alliance), QSA (Queer Straight Alliance), or affinity club. These are student-run organizations, often with a faculty advisor, that unite LGBTQIA+ and allied kids to build community and organize around issues impacting them in their schools, and serve as safe spaces for LGBTQIA+ students. Having an affinity club in their school can assist in protecting students from harassment based on sexual orientation or gender identity and improve school climates for all students in the long term. They can also have a positive, long-lasting influence on the mental, emotional, and academic well-being of LGBTQIA+ kids. Each GSA will have its own unique flavor, with the LGBTQIA+ kids and their faculty advisor collaborating on developing the right atmosphere. Some may have a very social aspect where the focus is about coming together for lunch and connecting with other LGBTQIA+ kids and allies. Others may create a place for support and talk, focusing on the myriad issues they face in school like bullying, discrimination, and harassment, but also on things like dating, LGBTQIA+ history, queer culture, and emerging identities. And some may take on activist tone where students take a leadership role to improve school climate through campaigns and events that raise awareness and change policies or practices in their schools. Whichever form it takes, a GSA can be a powerful and enlightening addition to any school environment.

As a parent, you can also take on more personal projects that reflect the needs you recognize in your own LGBTQIA+ child.

Projects you may wish to spearhead can come in many forms, including anti-slur campaigns, days of LGBTQIA+ sensitivity and awareness, teacher and staff trainings, and lobbying at school district meetings to address the needs of LGBTQIA+ students in the school setting. Perhaps you could lead the effort to bring an LGBTQIA+ Pride celebration to your school or community, knowing that June is officially known as Pride month around the world.

Speaking of Pride, you might find that you want to attend and participate in a Pride celebration in your community. Maybe it's just you, maybe it's you and your LGBTQIA+ kid, or maybe it's the entire family. This is another one of those moments where it is vital for you to check in with your LGBTQIA+ kid and formulate a plan to participate that feels comfortable and appropriate for all parties involved. From personal experience, I have found that attending a Pride celebration can be a life-changing experience. The joyous, affirming atmosphere can have a transformative effect on both parents and kids whose only exposure to LGBTQIA+ people and culture has been limited to their existing social circle and popular media. An experience like this can be the beginning of an even stronger bond between you and your LGBTQIA+ kid, as well as other family members, and foster expanded awareness and openness to the endless possibilities for expression and identity that are available for your kid to explore. Many of the families that I work with do eventually attend a Pride event, often with their kid, and for parents to witness how their LGBTQIA+ child lights up when they find themselves in an environment where the core essence of who they are is celebrated and affirmed has been profound for the entire family. Many parents come back in tears from these Pride events and report that it has been a long time since they have seen their kid this happy and comfortable with who they are as a member of the LGBTQIA+ community.

One thing to be cognizant of in relation to Pride events is that they are a celebration of gender and sexuality, which means that there will undoubtedly be tangible displays and symbols of sexuality, bodies, and gender expression. Parents should take into consideration the age and maturity of their LGBTQIA+ kid when considering attending a Pride celebration with them. Perhaps attend on your own one year and then take your kid the next, once you know what to expect. But also remember not to underestimate your kid. Whether you want to face it or not, your adolescent LGBTQIA+ kid is probably already far more knowledgeable than you imagine and may already be experimenting. Give them the opportunity to explore, experience, and make their own judgments.

While attending Pride can feel like a big public statement of support, I find that any well-meaning parent over time learns that the most challenging aspect of being an advocate is the day-to-day balance of wanting to make change in the world and wanting to keep things simple. As a parent, you will experience moments of harassment and discrimination simply for standing up and speaking out in support of the rights and needs of LGBTQIA+ people. As challenging as these moments can feel, remember that this is only a small taste of what your LGBTQIA+ kid may face every day. This awareness can make you more empathetic toward your LGBTQIA+ kid's coming-out journey and give context to many of the feelings and frustrations that they are (or aren't) expressing to you.

When you find yourself in situations where you are facing negative reactions or harassment, sometimes the best way to encourage allyship is to simply open up a conversation. If you hear or see something that's damaging toward your kid or the LGBTQIA+ community, consider asking for that person's thoughts and rationalizations for their opinions. Listening to them, however much you disagree with them, may create an opening for them to listen to you and consider another point of view. It won't always work, and you may find people so entrenched in their misguided beliefs and ignorance that further engagement is futile. Advocacy works the same way as so many of the other aspects of supporting and affirming your LGBTQIA+ kid on their coming-out journey. The most important thing is that you don't give up. You'll have ups and downs. You'll sometimes need to step back and recharge, let the negativity and occasional feelings of hopelessness pass. Advocacy requires you to become comfortable with being uncomfortable, which is perhaps one of the most courageous selfless acts you can ever pursue on behalf of your LGBTQIA+ kid.

It would be easy to say that you are always going to feel brave and step up to the plate, but that is not always a reasonable expectation to place on yourself. There are consequences to standing up and being a voice of LGBTQIA+ advocacy, and some days your voice will be primed, loud, and ready to respond while on others you may find your voice stifled and quiet. It's okay! You don't need to be the perfect parent advocate 24 hours a day, seven days a week. Choose "teachable moments'" where your efforts are likely to be heard and understood. Recognize that each act of advocacy will have its own cost in time, energy, and commitment. Your energy also shifts from day to day and moment to moment. Pay attention to your needs and give yourself a break when you need it. Know that you are on a journey of being the best parent advocate you can be and it's okay to pause and take a rest. You deserve it!

Remember that the moments where you need or choose to advocate can be big, high-profile projects, while others may be subtle and take the form of simple acts aimed at creating awareness. It is those smaller efforts that can sometimes feel the most uncomfortable to address. We've all been there, that moment when a close friend or colleague makes an offensive joke and suddenly your brain lights up with anxiety over how to handle the situation. Do you speak up and suddenly get labeled as the PC police or a "snowflake"? Do you remain quiet and keep the peace? Or do you just walk away feeling frustrated about not speaking up and addressing a statement you know is wrong and harmful? Exclusionary jokes and statements are serious and should be taken seriously. Responding to situations like these requires nuance and judgment. A productive approach is to look for a way to keep the conversation lighter, so that people don't shut down in anticipation of a lecture. As I have mentioned previously, I often approach these moments starting with the statement, "I don't know if you're aware, but those words you just used could be hurtful to someone in this room." This gives me a gentle opening in making the person aware, and often this approach is all that is needed for them to realize how their words can have an impact they may not have thought through.

Let's examine some possible approaches you can take as you develop your own personal strategy to respond to prejudicial, discriminatory, and anti-LGBTQIA+ comments, jokes, and statements you, your LGBTQIA+ kid, and your family may encounter. An approach that can help humanize the moment and lower the bar of conflict is to start the conversation about why, as a parent of an LGBTQIA+ kid, this conversation is important to you. Being willing to share why you are an ally can lower people's defenses and facilitate authentic conversation. Letting the other person know that their comment is hurtful to someone you love can assist them in better understanding the impact of their comment and help refocus the conversation. You can also approach the moment as an educational opportunity. Many times, people don't realize that their comments and jokes are making light of serious situations faced by real people, people they may even know and love. So, put your parent advocate education to use and share with the commentor the very real-world discriminations that LGBTQIA+ people, including your child, experience every day and how their comment may be part of that discrimination, harassment, and stereotyping.

As a parent advocate, that education I keep mentioning is not a one-and-done commitment. Advocacy is not just the memorization of a few dates and facts. It is an ongoing commitment to learning about the past, present, and future of the LGBTQIA+ community, ideally from those with lived experience. I encourage you to make a proactive effort to seek out information from community-created resources, and not assume that it is an LGBTQIA+ individual's responsibility to educate you. Instead, it is your responsibility to seek out the latest ideas, research, and realities to better advocate for the well-being of your LGBTQIA+ child.

I would also encourage that in your effort to speak out loud to raise awareness for your LGBTQIA+ child's safety and well-being you enter LGBTQIA+ spaces with humbleness and curiosity. When you approach an LGBTQIA+ community resource, remember that they have lived experience of the very discrimination and harassment that you are advocating against. Your job in that moment is to listen carefully and follow the lead of those community activists who have walked the very road your kid is journeying on right now. Learn without pressing, support without dominating. As an LGBTQIA+ person, I personally welcome you into my world and encourage open conversations focused on the shared goal of making the world safer and welcoming to all LGBTQIA+ kids everywhere.

As we come to the end of this chapter, I encourage you once again to take a moment to digest this information and discern for yourself how you want to approach the role of parent advocate. Some of you will be ready, willing, and able to take on the mantle of public advocacy, while others may choose a quieter, more personal approach to supporting your LGBTQIA+ kids. Each of us will find our own authentic path, and that authentic approach will become your own unique superpower as a parent advocate for your LGBTQIA+ child. Know that your allyship means a lot to all of us in the LGBTQIA+ community and that we cheer you on when you take the risk and speak up and speak out.

Questions for contemplation

1. How does the prospect of being an advocate for your LGBT-QIA+ child feel?
2. How does the prospect of being an advocate for the LGBT-QIA+ community at large feel to you?
3. Who are you most concerned about having conversations about LGBTQIA+ advocacy with?
4. What feelings arise when you consider speaking out at your child's school about creating and implementing LGBT-QIA+-affirming policies?
5. Are you ready, willing, and able to attend a Pride event? And what will you wear?

LGBTQIA+ FAQs and SOS Help Guide

My child just told me they are...gay, bisexual, lesbian, pansexual, trans-gender, non-binary... What do I do?

The most supportive and powerful reaction you can have to your child coming out is to simply hug them tight and let them know that you love them. You will hear me advise this approach through-out this book. The reason is that at the moment your kid comes out to you, what they need most in the world is to feel love from you as their parent. This moment of coming out has been spinning around in their mind and heart for a long time, and one of the biggest fears that all LGBTQIA+ kids identify is the fear that you, as their parent, will no longer love them. You may have lots of thoughts and feelings you need to work out for yourself in this process, but at the moment they share with you this delicate, fragile facet of their identity, simply love them, and then love them some more.

I am always worried about the safety and well-being of my LGBTQIA+ child.

Congratulations! You are a parent! Worrying about the safety of your kid is part of the parent contract, and when your kid comes out and you learn all about the new risks they may be exposed to, it gets even more challenging. Breathe, talk with your partner, talk with your kid. Find out which of your fears are based in reality and which ones are based on misinformation, propaganda, or outdated thinking. For the ones that turn out to be valid, work with your kid on creating a safety plan in case they need one in the future. If it isn't a valid fear, give yourself some space and time to move through the anxiety and educate yourself, talking with other members of your support network such as a therapist, support group, or other parents who may be able to guide you through this fear.

I'm pretty sure my kid is...lesbian, gay, bisexual, transgender...but doesn't seem to want to come out to me. What do I do?

If your kid is not ready to come out to you, I beg you not to try and out them. This applies to all identities under the LGBTQIA+ banner. Your kid will come out to you when they are good and ready. Ultimately, it is their process, and your job is to be informed and supportive, not to push. Create an affirming energy in your household in regard to all sexual orientations and gender identities so your kid knows that their family is a safe and supportive space. They may come out tomorrow or they may not come out until they are an adult. That is their choice, and the best you can do is to love and affirm them until they are ready to speak openly about their LGBTQIA+ identity.

What did I do to make them LGBTQIA+?

Nothing. As a parent, it is easy to fall into a trap that somehow you did something wrong that made them this way. Your kid is

LGBTQIA+ because that is who they authentically are, and the coming-out process is simply them owning that powerful identity. On a deeper level, I want you to pause for a moment and chew on the thought that there must be something to blame for your kid's LGBTQIA+ identity. At its core, that thought means that you may view being LGBTQIA+ as a bad thing. Where might that thinking have come from? Is it possible that your upbringing and family life have created an anti-LGBTQIA+ bias that you were not even aware of until it showed up right in your own house? Check yourself, see where those concepts may have developed, and then see how you can move on from them. As a fabulous, openly queer man, I can tell you that there is nothing wrong with owning my queerness and nothing was the cause of this amazing aspect of who I am.

Will an affirming LGBTQIA+ therapist make my kid LGBTQIA+ as well?

I would suggest that this is some of the same thinking as the previous question. Once again, nobody has the power to make your kid LGBTQIA+, they simply are. A trained affirming therapist will assist your kid in finding their way to expressing that identity in the healthiest, most authentic manner for them. I often have parents ask me, "Are you going to turn my kid gay? Trans? Lesbian?" I inform them that no therapist has that power, just as no therapist can turn their kid straight or cisgender.

The extended family won't use my kid's affirmed pronouns.

If your kid has shared openly about their name and pronouns, it needs to become a family cause to gently but firmly correct and inform those family members who are having a challenge with this change. Use simple corrections such as, "Their pronouns are..." or, "You mean..." reminding them of your kid's correct name. It doesn't have to be an angry or frustrating moment. Keep it consistent and calm. Talk openly about how much it hurts you and your child when they misgender or misname them. Talk openly about the challenges you had in making this adjustment and how you have grown through this process. If there is adamant refusal to use your kid's name and pronouns, sit down with your kid and see if they would feel safer not having interactions with that family member. Then follow through with their wishes and set some boundaries that feel appropriate for all of you.

My gay son wants to have a sleepover with a boy he is dating. What am I supposed to do?

I guess that depends on your family rules about sleepovers for all of your kids. It has been a constant surprise to me over the years of working with LGBTQIA+ youth and their families how challenging it can be when their LGBTQIA+ kid wants to have their partner spend the night. Instead of relying on the rules they have set up for their cisgender straight children, they suddenly feel they must create an entirely new rule book for their LGBTQIA+ child. If it is okay for any of your children to have partners sleep over when they reach a certain age, it needs to be okay for all your children to have sleepovers when they reach that age. Implement the family rules consistently and you will be creating an affirming environment in your home.

My transgender son tells me he is attracted to girls. Is he straight or gay?

The short answer to that question is that ultimately it is his decision to proclaim his sexual orientation and yours to support that declaration. The more complex answer is to understand that sexual orientation and gender identity are separate processes of identity development, but they can often become intertwined as your kid is figuring out their authentic self. A trans man is a person who was assigned female at birth but grows to understand that they are male. As any trans person moves toward their affirmed gender, questions of attraction will come to the forefront. Rather than trying to categorize your kid in a black and white binary sexual orientation, leave room for them to unveil themselves as they learn more about themselves and their attractions. They will appreciate the freedom, space, and support this offers as they explore these questions for themselves.

My transgender/non-binary child wants to start hormone-affirming treatment. What do I do?

I have found over the years that many of the parents I work with are able to support their trans/non-binary kid as long as that support involves social transition, names, pronouns, clothing, grooming, makeup, and hairstyle changes. When the question of medical transitions comes up, usually the implementation of hormone-affirming treatments, this is when parents get a little panicky. Think about it this way. Your job as a parent has been to keep your kid safe all these years, and now they want to introduce chemicals that are going to change the look and essence of their body so they can actively and physically reconcile who they know themselves to be on the inside with who they appear to be on the outside. This movement into medical procedures will be really challenging for you but, ultimately, supporting these procedures is providing for the safety and well-being of your child on a mental, physical, and emotional level. There is a deep beauty and joy in witnessing and supporting the medical transition of your kid. When you as a parent move through your own fear and concern, you will be amazed at the mental and emotional growth that your kid will experience as their body comes into alignment with who they authentically are as a person.

My daughter told us she is a lesbian, but I suspect she is not and is just being influenced by her friends and social media. What should I do?

This is a very interesting question that comes up a lot, especially as the power of social media in all our lives continues to evolve and grow. Parents often come to me and state that they feel their kid has been watching a lot of LGBTQIA+ content and they now think of themselves that way. I like to posit the opposite hypothesis, that they were searching out a lot of LGBTQIA+ content because they were trying to find people like them. In the initial moments of wondering if they are LGBTQIA+, most kids feel ostracized by their peers, school, and family. They feel like an outsider in most situations and wonder what is wrong with them. By searching out movies, TV shows, books, TikTok channels, and other forms of media where they can witness their identity being expressed and celebrated, they begin to gain a more assured sense of who they are and how they want to express themselves in the world. Ultimately, there is nothing you "should" do, but instead affirm your support and join with them in love and curiosity as they explore their sexual orientation.

How does my kid know they are gay if they have never been in a hetero-sexual relationship?

Please pardon my directness here, but how did you know you were straight if you never had a gay relationship? Got it? Ultimately, we don't need to date everyone to know where our attractions lie. Instead, it is a more intrinsic sensation we feel inside that guides our interest and attractions. You kid is walking through a world where every moment of every day tells them that straight is the way, and it takes a lot of bravery and strength to push back against this social pressure and find and own their unique sexual orientation.

If my kid is bisexual, why can't they just choose to be in a straight relationship?

The thing that most people miss about bisexuality and pansexuality is that the capacity to feel attraction to multiple genders doesn't mean that bisexual and pansexual people can control who they are attracted to any more than people who are attracted to a single gender. It also doesn't mean that since they have the capacity to feel attraction toward multiple genders that they are attracted to everyone. Attraction is a complex and nuanced emotional, intellectual, and physical response that is influenced by countless hardwired aspects of a person's personality, life experience, and core identity. Asking a bisexual or pansexual person to limit their attractions to a socially accepted norm is like saying you can only listen to classical music for the rest of your life even though you enjoy many different genres of music. Your kid's attractions may vary as they move through different relationships, and there is no single or right way for them to focus their attractions, most certainly not because of biases or beliefs that you or society try to impose on them. If you are feeling this way about your bisexual or pansexual kid, I would encourage you to look at your own feelings and biases about their sexual orientation and determine whether you are actually capable of supporting and affirming their identity at this time. If not, seeking out education, guidance, and support from resources like a trained affirming therapist, community support groups, or informed affirming friends would be a positive next step.

My religious community says that they can help my child not be LGBT-QIA+. What should I do?

The first thing for you as a parent to do if you hear this kind of suggestion from anyone is to say no, loudly and forcefully. Conversion therapy is an incredibly harmful practice that some religious groups use as a means to influence LGBTQIA+ kids and their families to "change" their child's gender identity or sexual orientation. These practices are painful, abusive, and harmful, and leave people with permanent psychological and sometimes physical damage.

Be aware that these so-called conversion practices may be referred to by various names to make them sound gentler, more legitimate, more therapeutic, or more appealing. This is just marketing and does not diminish the danger these abusive practices pose to your kid and your family.

These names include:

- Reparative therapy
- Conversion therapy
- Sexual orientation change efforts (SOCE)
- Sexual reorientation efforts
- Sexual attraction fluidity exploration in therapy (SAFE-T)
- Ex-gay ministry
- Eliminating, reducing, or decreasing frequency or intensity of unwanted same-sex attraction (SSA)
- Promoting healthy sexuality
- Sexual addictions and disorders counseling
- Sexuality counseling.

These dangerous and discredited techniques have been rejected by every major psychological and medical organization and yet are still practiced in many places. I beg you to reject these approaches even if you are having challenges affirming your kid's gender identity or sexual orientation. As a parent, you want to do the best for your child, and I cannot stress enough that these "reparative" practices are dangerous and harmful for them.

Won't being LGBTQIA+ make my kid's life harder for them?

I have to confess, when I came out to my mom one of her first concerns was that my life was going to be more difficult as a queer man. I understood her concerns and also was aware that coming out was the most authentic way for me to lead my life. Yes, there have been challenges and moments where I have felt unsafe. Yet those few moments do not outweigh the powerful life I have experienced as an out and proud queer man. With more and more visibility in the LGBTQIA+ community including people in politics, sports, arts, and education, your child has the opportunity to live a beautiful life, with your support.

Why is my child choosing to be LGBTQIA+?

The idea of your kid making a choice to be LGBTQIA+ is not an accurate understanding of their journey. Their sexual orientation and gender identity are who they are and have been from birth. The only choice they are making is how and when to express that identity. Gender identity and sexual orientation emerge quite early in life and are simply a natural aspect of who your kid is. The coming-out process is a multi-layered journey, and I like to picture it as your LGBTQIA+ kid removing the mask and the armor they have been wearing and inviting you in to see exactly who they have been all along.

Resources

LGBTQIA+ family resources

Advocates for Youth: advocatesforyouth.org

Ali Forney Center: aliforneycenter.org

Bisexual Resource Center: biresource.net

COLAGE: colage.org

Family Acceptance Project: familyproject.sfsu.edu

Family Equality: FamilyEquality.org

Gender Spectrum: genderspectrum.org

GLAAD: glaad.org

GLBT Near Me: glbtnearme.org

GLSEN (Gay, Lesbian, and Straight Education Network): glsen.org

GSA Network: gsanetwork.org

Human Rights Campaign: hrc.org

It Gets Better Project: itgetsbetter.org

Lambda Legal: lambdalegal.org

LGBT Foundation: lgbt.foundation

National Black Justice Coalition: nbjc.org

National Center for Transgender Equality: transequality.org

National LGBTQ Task Force: thetaskforce.org

National Queer Asian Pacific Islander Alliance (NQAPIA): nqapia.org

PFLAG: pflag.org

Scarleteen: scarleteen.com

The Trevor Project: thetrevorproject.org

Trans Lifeline: translifeline.org

Trans Youth Equality Center: transyouthequality.org

True Colors United: truecolorsunited.org

LGBTQIA+ religious support organizations

Affirmations (LDS): affirmation.org

Association of Welcoming & Affirming Baptists (Baptist): awab.org

Dignity USA (Catholic): dignityusa.org

Disciples LGBTQ+ Alliance (Disciples of Christ): disciplesallianceq.org

Eshel (Jewish: Orthodox): eshelonline.org

JQ International (Jewish): jqinternational.org

Keshet (Jewish): keshetonline.org

Metropolitan Community Church (Christian): mccchurch.org

More Light Presbyterians (Presbyterian): mlp.org

Muslims for Progressive Values (Muslim): mpvusa.org/lgbtqi-resources

Rainbodhi (Buddhism): rainbodhi.org

Reconciling Ministries (Methodist): rmnetwork.org

Reconciling Works (Lutheran): reconcilingworks.org

Unitarian Universalist Association: uua.org/LGBTQ

United Church of Christ (UCC): openandaffirming.org/ona/find

International

GATE (Global Action for Trans Equality): gate.ngo

IGLYO (International Lesbian, Gay, Bisexual, Transgender, Queer and Intersex Youth & Student Organisation): iglyo.com

ILGA (International Lesbian, Gay, Bisexual, Trans and Intersex Association): ILGA.org

LGBT Ireland: lgbt.ie

No More Fear Foundation: nomorefearfoundation.org

OutRight International: outrightinternational.org

Rainbow Families: rainbowfamilies.com.au

Acknowledgments

At the start of this book, I described myself as your LGBTQIA+ guide on this magnificent journey of understanding, supporting, and affirming your LGBTQIA+ child during their coming-out process. Just as I hope I have been a support for you, there are many people who have been a support for me on the journey of creating this book.

I want to start by thanking the crew at Jessica Kingsley Publishers, especially my amazing editor Andrew, who from our very first Zoom chat created an affirming and supportive environment for this book to be nurtured and developed. Andrew understood the importance of this book to me and assisted me in shaping it into the resource you now have in your hands.

Before it even got into Andrew's hands, though, it went through the power copyediting of my secret grammar ninja, Barbara, who caught all of the misspellings and grammar oopsies, and supported me in my deep desire to use the Oxford comma. As the mom of a gay child, she also helped me see the book through a mom's eyes and find those words that could provide the support a parent would need.

Thanks to Traci, James, Elisa, Kim, and Liz for providing me with a fresh set of eyes to tighten things up and make sure the messages of support for our LGBTQIA+ kids were accurate, current, and on point.

Thanks to Lisa for providing us a home while this book was being written.

This book would not be possible without the many brave families who have come through my office door and honored me with their trust, confidence, fear, anxiety, and confusion as we've worked together to create an affirming coming-out journey. This book also would not have been possible without the training, consultation, and support that I have received over the years from my fellow therapists, consultants, and teachers, who always push me to learn more and bring my best work forward.

Finally, words are so inadequate to express my deepest gratitude to my loving husband, Martin. He has been a guiding light through this entire process, and the book you see in front of you would not exist without his support, wisdom, critical editing eye, expansive vocabulary, and deep love that helps me to be my best self as we travel along the road of life together. I owe you a vacation!

Index